beyond
the
best
dressed

Running Press
Hachette Book Group
1290 Avenue of the Americas, New York, NY 10104
www.runningpress.com
@Running_Press

Printed in China

First Edition: February 2022

Published by Running Press, an imprint of Perseus Books, LLC, a subsidiary of Hachette Book Group, Inc. The Running Press name and logo is a trademark of the Hachette Book Group.

The Hachette Speakers Bureau provides a wide range of authors for speaking events. To find out more, go to www.hachettespeakersbureau.com or call (866) 376-6591.

The publisher is not responsible for websites (or their content) that are not owned by the publisher.

Print book cover and interior design by Susan Van Horn.

Page iv graphic from Getty Images contributer carduus/DigitalVision Vectors

Library of Congress Control Number: 2021943384

ISBNs: 978-0-7624-7550-6 (hardcover), 978-0-7624-7549-0 (ebook)

RRD-S

10 9 8 7 6 5 4 3 2 1

beyond the best dressed

A CULTURAL HISTORY OF
THE MOST GLAMOROUS,
RADICAL, AND SCANDALOUS
OSCAR FASHION

esther zuckerman

Illustrated by
montana forbes

RUNNING PRESS
PHILADELPHIA

contents

introduction

VER THE COURSE OF NEARLY 100 YEARS, THE rituals of the Academy Awards and its attire have been chronicled and codified. A certain level of glam in one's presentation is expected, if not demanded, and now supported by a cottage industry of stylists and squads who are at the beck and call of nominees and presenters to turn them from mere mortals into gods and goddesses. For those of us at home on our couches, there are traditions too: Turning on E! in the middle of the day to watch the hours-long red carpet coverage before switching to the official telecast; logging onto Getty Images to get a closer look at the detailing on the gowns; reading websites like The Fug Girls or Tom and Lorenzo the next day for expert analysis of the fashion.

The Oscars have often been written off as a frivolous, out-of-touch, navel-gazing celebration *of* Hollywood *by* Hollywood, but for better or worse they have become a pop culture bell-wether, as much for their spectacle as for their substance. Only some of the most memorable Oscar moments have anything to do with the movies in contention. And many have more to do with clothes than anything else. For every *Moonlight* beats *La La Land* shocker, there's a Björk swan dress.

Fashion and the Oscars have become inextricably linked, particularly for the women who attend the event, but there's more to the question "who are you wearing?" than is commonly assumed. What a woman chooses to put on her body for argu-ably the highest-profile event of the year can be a statement of intent, an acceptance of status in the pantheon of celebrity, or a rebuke of the role she's been assigned. Her pick carries a lot of weight. If she wins, that can be the image of her that lands in the history books. It matters.

Talking about fashion devoid of context can be tricky. In 2015, the #AskHerMore campaign began as an effort to get commentators to stop asking women at the Oscars and other awards shows substance-free questions solely about their clothing. But, even though reporting on red carpets is often fizzy (and occasionally even demeaning), the substance of the fashion is not. Style is a statement, and Oscar-wear especially speaks volumes, whether you're Joan Crawford accepting a trophy in a nightgown from bed or Edy Williams baring as much as possible on the pathway to the Dorothy Chandler Pavilion.

You can't talk about the Oscars without talking about politics: After all, the notorious MGM studio head Louis B. Mayer invented the Academy as a way to stop the formation of unions among Hollywood's workers in the late 1920s. His notion was that if he established this organization to celebrate the stars and artisans of the studio system, they wouldn't ask for rights and benefits from their bosses. His ploy didn't work, but the Oscars did, and became a cause for celebration and an arbiter of the industry's status quo. It's not as if the Oscars celebrate the most daring films released every year. They often uphold old-fashioned ideas of what Hollywood is supposed to look like: white, wealthy, and unadventurous.

In the early days Oscar fashion was often dictated by studios. The honored women would wear outfits by the costume designers who had dressed them for their films. Couture started to enter the conversation by the 1950s and '60s, and by the 1990s, when Joan and Melissa Rivers began their reign of comedic terror over on E!, the business of who was wearing what was as much of an industry as the awards themselves. "Joan Rivers showed up, 'Who did your dress?' And before you know it all the European designers were offering clothes for nothing, which always made me laugh," the legendary designer Bob Mackie told me in an interview for this book. "Here are these people making millions of dollars being in movies: They love to get a free dress."

The Rivers' era was marked by nastiness. Make what they considered to be an ill-advised sartorial decision and you would get mercilessly mocked. In a 2016 piece for the *New York Times*, the writer Haley Mlotek issued a searing takedown of carpet culture. "Red-carpet commentators enforce a code of conduct that pretends to be about fashion but is really about control," she wrote. "Appointed by television networks and glossy magazines, these people don't reward self-expression. They're implementing a now-entrenched notion of what makes a winning red-carpet dress: a glorified prom dress with a couture tag."

Hollywood's reckoning following the #MeToo movement has seemingly ushered in an age of commentary that is, at least on its surface, less cruelly critical of women and their choices, regarding fashion or otherwise. In an age of positivity online, worst-dressed lists don't hold the same cache as they once did. Outfits that were once derided have received waves of reappraisals. Extravagance is cheered rather than admonished.

But the Oscars these days are known as much for their sparkles as they are for their sins, whether nasty sexism or the racism implicit in the overwhelming whiteness of the winners. April Reign was watching the nominations in 2015 when she tweeted #OscarsSoWhite, a hashtag that evolved into a movement that's still ongoing. To combat the long-entrenched racism of the institution, the Academy began attempting to expand its membership. And, yet, a retrograde movie like *Green Book* still won Best Picture in 2019, making the case that the younger, more diverse membership hadn't made much of an impact yet.

This is all to say, if you look at Oscar style in a bubble, you're missing the bigger picture. Gowns are often so much more than just gowns. And frequently they aren't even gowns. (Some of the women I write about in this book opted for pants.) These ensembles, arranged chronologically, offer insight into the women they adorn and the world they occupy. Mary Pickford's jeweled drop-waist signals a woman who was about to mold what would become a Hollywood tradition in her own image. Rita Moreno obtained her patterned dress at a low point in her life and proved she was still standing when she donned it decades later. Jane Fonda's black suit in 1972 echoed her activism. Diablo Cody's leopard-print sheath kept true to her riot grrrl spirit. Zendaya boldly wore locs and was met with uninformed criticism, but both her look and her response to the naysayers heralded the arrival of a new star. There are the most famous pieces of Oscar attire, of course—Audrey Hepburn's white quasi-Givenchy and Halle Berry's embroidered Elie Saab—but there are also others that nonetheless have their own strange, fascinating narratives even if they aren't as immediately recognizable. And through the lens of Oscar fashion, you can also examine the racism and sexism that has plagued Hollywood since its birth.

The Oscars are ingrained in the American imagination, and so are the clothes that are worn to these ceremonies. Garments tell stories. They tell stories about what kinds of people and bodies get celebrated; they mark pivotal moments in lives. They can demonstrate the passage of time and the mores of an entire era. What a woman wears is everything, and yet she is not defined by what she wears. This is never truer than on what is colloquially known as Hollywood's biggest night. There's so much more than just "Best Dressed."

A QUICK NOTE

Dating the Oscars is a complicated matter. Do you ascribe a ceremony the year in which it takes place or the year in which the films it is honoring came out? There are some die-hard Oscars aficionados who believe the latter is correct, but for the purpose of this exercise, since I am focusing on the event itself, the former is more appropriate. When I refer to, say, the 2020 Oscars I'm talking about the Oscars honoring the films of 2019 that happened in 2020. Make sense?

mary pickford

(1930)

I N ONE OF THE FIRST IMAGES WE HAVE OF A BEST Actress winner, she is not wearing a gown. When Janet Gaynor accepted the inaugural Oscar for Best Actress in 1929, she was photographed taking the award from Douglas Fairbanks wearing a sweater with a plain white skirt and a scarf loosely tied around her chest. Her socks protrude out of her laced-up loafers. It's strikingly casual for an event that has since become synonymous with glamour, and the picture was not even captured at the actual ceremony. No one knows what Gaynor wore to the party, which looked very different from the lavish ceremony we have come to expect these days. The awards were a banquet with dinner and dancing. A committee of five judges picked the winners.

It would take a while for the Academy Awards to blossom into their current hoopla, but if there was anyone responsible for hurrying along that process it was the second Best Actress winner, Mary Pickford. The prevailing image of Mary and her prize is a complete 180 from that of Janet. Whereas Janet is seen demurely accepting her trophy, Mary's is set on a table next to her. She stands, lording over it, one hand on her waist. Her gown, a drop waist emblematic of the times, is detailed with jewels around her hips. She wears two shimmering brace-lets and three strings of pearls. Behind her, on a chair, sits an overcoat of some sort, lined with fur. She stares into the cam-era, her gaze confident, a little beauty mark under her cheek. The trophy seemed to loom over Janet. Here, it's Mary looming over Oscar.

The Academy Awards—in all their splendor and scandal—as we know them would not exist without Mary Pickford, one of the most intriguing figures of early Hollywood. One can argue that Pickford established the tradition of dressing up for the occasion. She also launched what has been deemed the first Oscar campaign, setting the precedent that the actual best performance doesn't always walk away with the prize.

Watching *Coquette*, the film that nabbed Pickford the prize for the 1928-1929 Oscar season, is a chore. She plays Norma, a Southern belle, who falls in love with the wrong man. Her dis-approving father gravely injures her beau and is put on trial for murder. In order to save the life of her dad, Norma must slander the name of her dead boyfriend. Pickford, in her first talking role, is melodramatic and swooning, emphasizing every word. The story is slight, and the film is filled with insidious, racist imagery of the early 20th-century South, including a "mammy" stereotype of a character, who cradles Norma as she weeps over her fate.

Like so many other Oscar winners who would follow, Pickford's choice of star vehicle in *Coquette* was seen as a risk and an attempt to change her image in the public eye. Born Gladys Smith in Toronto, Pickford's rise was a rags-to-riches story, the stuff of Hollywood dreams. She started as a teenager on Broadway, before auditioning for director D. W. Griffith on the demand of her mother, who, eyeing the bigger salary movies had to offer, wanted her to make it in pictures. (Pickford initially believed that would be a step down in stature, according to her biographer Scott Eyman.) Pickford was a performer who refused to settle, who was constantly negotiating herself a bigger piece of the pie. She was instrumental in the founding of United Artists Studio, alongside her second husband Douglas Fairbanks, and was one of only three women responsible for starting the Academy. She bought the rights to projects she wanted to make, charting her own career path.

When she starred in *Coquette*, she was also frustrated. She was consistently cast as children well into her 30s. She wore her hair in long ringlets and had a knack for embodying urchins and brats. Multiple times she took on dual roles, like when she played mother and son in *Little Lord Fauntleroy* and the titular paralyzed protagonist and an orphaned servant in *Stella Maris*. After her mother, who had served as almost a proto-momager, died, Mary wanted to move on. So in 1928, she cut her hair. "They had been my making, those curls, and my unmaking too," she wrote in an unpublished autobiography, per her official foundation. "They had given my pictures a badge of respectability. They prohibited me from playing anything in the slightest degree censorable. . . . Mothers trusted those curls as they trusted their own consciences. Between that restriction and the weight of the curls, there was little left for me to do and very little ground that I could cover. . . . I played a little girl for the last time. I was determined now, as I had never been before, to close the door on my screen childhood and to be my age, or something near it."

Her adoring public felt betrayed. Think of it like a jazz age version of the scandal that hit the WB series *Felicity* when Keri Russell sheared her curly locks, except in Pickford's case the chop was such big news it made the front page of the *New York Times*.

Coquette was a transition out of kid roles. Suddenly, armed with her bob, she was playing a fallen woman with sex appeal. Her performance was tepidly received. While critic

Mordaunt Hall of the *New York Times* wrote that she saved the movie with her "earnest efforts," he also added: "Miss Pickford herself chose to appear in *Coquette*, but whether the role of Norma Beasant is suited to her is a matter of opinion. She is pretty, but on the screen with close-ups, she looks a trifle too mature and too wise for the part of a young, impetuous girl." She had outgrown kid parts but was considered too mature for this adult role.

Not that reviews were going to stop her from winning an Oscar. She invited the Academy's Board of Judges over for tea at Pickfair, the famed estate she shared with Fairbanks, and pled her case. They acquiesced. It's hard to blame Mary for these tactics, at least not entirely. This was the Wild West of the Oscars and she wasn't exactly breaking any rules. Mary's bribery led the Academy to open up voting to all members, but the tradition of doing whatever it took to win would continue to be a part of the festivities for decades to come, with the likes of David O. Selznick and—yes—the since-disgraced Harvey Weinstein leading the charge. Mary was savvy. She knew this business was political, so she threw a party and dressed up for the occasion.

How did she acquire her Oscar dress and what thought went into it? In *Made for Each Other: Fashion and the Academy Awards*, Bronwyn Cosgrave speculates that it was part of a collection of gowns Pickford had acquired in Europe while she was plotting her Oscar triumph with *Coquette*. Her purchases became a minor scandal when they were held up in customs after officials believed she declared them for too small a value, which she had only done because she got them at cheaper prices thanks to her fame. The dress in question was "Fragonard blue," one of Pickford's favorite colors, according to Cosgrave, and was possibly the work of couturier Jeanne Lanvin. Still, little is known about its actual provenance, only that it looked absolutely lovely. Looking at that image of her, practically glimmering, you can see the future of the organization and the party she helped create. Pickford is the ultimate example of an outfit in which, if you look beyond the glitz, there's a lot more going on.

But Pickford also established another trend for actresses who win Oscars: the notion that this triumph is also the closing of a door. One of the persistent myths of the Oscars is that, for a woman, winning can be a career killer. It's sexist, and largely incorrect. And yet Pickford only made three more films after *Coquette*. By 1933 her career in front of the camera was basically over. Audiences didn't accept her playing a grown woman. She said, "I left the screen. The little girl made me. I wasn't waiting for the little girl to kill me."

hattie
mcdaniel

(1940)

HATTIE MCDANIEL MUST HAVE LIKED GARDENIAS. When she became the first Black person to ever win an Oscar, she wore a gardenia pinned to her hair. A shawl of gardenias cascaded over her shoulder, accentuating the rhinestone studded jacket she wore with her dress, which has been described as "aqua" or "turquoise." She also put gardenias in her will. In describing how she wanted to be buried, she wrote: "I desire a white casket and a white shroud; white gardenias in my hair and in my hands, together with a white gardenia blanket and a pillow of red roses." These flowers were also how Mo'Nique paid tribute to McDaniel at the same event 70 years later. "The reason why I have on this royal blue dress is because it's the color that Hattie McDaniel wore in 1940 when she accepted her Oscar," Mo'Nique said. "The reason why I have this gardenia in my hair, it is the flower that Hattie McDaniel wore when she accepted her Oscar. So for you, Miss Hattie

McDaniel, I feel you all over me." In Rita Dove's poem, "Hattie McDaniel Arrives at the Coconut [sic] Grove," she describes the actress "in aqua and ermine, gardenias / scaling her left sleeve in a spasm of scent."

Just why McDaniel chose gardenias is harder to determine. She certainly wasn't the only star at the time to wear them. Billie Holiday had made them her signature flower. In 1939, the same year that McDaniel starred in *Gone with the Wind*, a film that lionized the white antebellum South, Holiday recorded "Strange Fruit," a dirge about lynching that is considered one of the greatest civil rights songs in history.

To talk about Hattie McDaniel's appearance at the 1940 Oscars is to reckon with America's racism broadly speaking, as well as a film that is still both wildly popular and wildly insidious. McDaniel's win was a triumphant moment for Hollywood, one which the industry used to praise itself as progressive, and yet it also remains a bitter reminder of what kind of roles Black women are lauded for playing. The way the image of McDaniel at the Cocoanut Grove, an all-white club where the awards were then held, has passed through time and been echoed by those who have followed in her footsteps is a testament to her legacy, but that legacy is complicated. McDaniel remains both a trailblazer and a divisive figure in the annals of both Hollywood and U.S. history.

McDaniel was born the daughter of Henry McDaniel, a former slave and Union soldier. Her siblings got into performing before she did, but she eventually joined what became the family business. She worked in minstrel shows, and in her comedy, according to biographer Jill Watts, she "bravely attacked the central female character of white racist fantasies: The plantation Mammy." "Mammy" is also the name of McDaniel's most famous role, one with which she would forever be associated.

In June 2020, following the deaths of George Floyd, Breonna Taylor, and other Black men and women killed in racially motivated incidents, there were calls to take *Gone with the Wind* off the streaming service HBO Max. Warner Media temporarily removed the film, and when it came back it had a new introduction from Jacqueline Stewart, a Black film historian and Turner Classic Movies host. As Stewart explains, there was never a time when *Gone with the Wind* wasn't controversial. The debate and furor has existed since Margaret Mitchell published her tome glorifying the Confederacy, and powerful film producer David O. Selznick jumped on the chance to adapt it. Even then, Selznick tried to tamp down the fury he knew the project would inspire by consulting the NAACP.

McDaniel fought hard for the role of Mammy. She told the *Los Angeles Times Sunday Magazine* she had read the book three times. By that time, she was known in Hollywood, having appeared in films like *Show Boat*, and was already a polarizing figure in the Black press for her participation in the white system that kept Black performers in denigrating roles like maids and slaves. This criticism would continue through the highly publicized filming of *Gone with the Wind*, during which time one Black journalist wrote that McDaniel's role "means about $2,000 for Miss McDaniel in individual advancement . . . [and] nothing in racial advancement." How McDaniel was portrayed in the press depended on what press you were reading. As Watts describes, a journalist and friend of Mitchell's, Susan Myrick, who was also a dialect tutor on set, wrote that "she is being a Mammy in real life," a description that was meant to seem charming to the white readers but was really an insidious conflation of performer and material. McDaniel countered that characterization in an interview with the *New York Amsterdam News* after the film was out and criticism of her performance had mounted, arguing that she played Mammy as "the brave efficient type of womanhood which, building a race, mothered Booker T. Washington, George Carver, Robert Morton, and Mary McLeod Bethune." The *LA Times Sunday Magazine* profile, which came out about a month before the Oscars, was peppered with racist language, describing a young McDaniel as a "pickaninny," but also portraying her as a savvy, ambitious businesswoman: "She has a head for business that's as hard as a rock and hasn't been the least bit turned by what they call success in Hollywood language."

McDaniel knew her worth. She was the one who advocated that Selznick submit her performance for an Academy Award nomination, but her appearance at the Oscars was once again reflective of the white supremacy that surrounded her. Her presence was an opportunity for Hollywood to quite literally applaud itself for its progressiveness and inclusion—the audience clapped when she entered. At the same time, the event took place at a segregated venue where McDaniel was relegated to a seat in the back of the room. The famous gossip columnist Louella Parsons wrote that: "If you had seen her face when she walked up to the platform and took the gold trophy, you would have had the choke in your voice that all of us had when Hattie, hair trimmed with gardenias, face alight, and dressed to the queen's taste, accepted the honor in one of the finest speeches ever given on the Academy floor." Parsons's description of McDaniel's outfit is laden with the condescending, racist language of respectability. This woman, who was winning for playing a slave and subjugated during the very event at which she was being honored, was "dressed to the queen's taste." The column is indicative of the kind of self-congratulatory white press that surrounded McDaniel's win. Sure, Hollywood had made a film so loving in its depiction of the American South that it glorified the Confederacy, but it was also able to anoint the first Black winner of the highest honor in the field.

The speech Parsons referenced has long been rumored to have been written for McDaniel by the studio, which is not to discredit what the accomplishment must have meant to her, or the genuine emotion in her voice. "I shall always hold it as a beacon for whatever I may be able to do in the future," McDaniel said at the microphone. "I sincerely hope I shall always be a credit to my race and to the motion picture industry. My heart is too full to tell you just how I feel."

But McDaniel wasn't allowed to do much more in that "motion picture industry." Under contract first with Selznick and then with Warner Bros. she was relegated to the same domestic roles into which she had always been forced. Even her final request would not be acted upon until years later. She asked, yes, to be buried with gardenias, but also in the Hollywood Forever Cemetery. When she died in 1952, it was still segregated. Her Oscar, the plaque given to supporting performers at the time, was lost despite her wishes to have it donated to Howard University.

All those years later Mo'Nique would echo McDaniel's outfit, wear a gardenia in her hair, and find herself in a remarkably similar position. She won Best Supporting Actress for her role in *Precious*, playing a character that some would say exacerbated stereotypes of poor Black women. After her victory she, too, did not go on to greater success in Hollywood. She found her career in freefall because of her insistence on speaking bluntly and her refusal to play into the games of power players.

Hattie McDaniel and her gardenias changed the Academy Awards forever, but the Academy Awards were forever reluctant to advance beyond 1940. Those gardenias may have long ago wilted, but their scent still lingers today.

dress codes

HOW IS ONE SUPPOSED TO DRESS FOR THE ACADEMY Awards? In the 21st century there's a general, if imperfect answer. The stars come to the Oscars meticulously groomed by professional stylists. They receive gowns and suits from the biggest fashion houses and jewels from Harry Winston and the like. In the vaguest sense, going to the Oscars means dressing to the nines however best you can, whether you're the latest ingenue nominated for Best Actress or the director of the winner for Best Animated Short. The fashion designer responsible for Björk's infamous swan dress once said: "With the Oscars, there's a uniform, like the police." These days there's a sense that attendees can interpret the formalwear requirement at will. Costume design nominee Jenny Beavan wore a bedazzled motorcycle jacket in 2016. Figure skater Adam Rippon put on a formal harness in 2018. Cher has gone to the ceremony baring skin on multiple occasions. (She's Cher. She can.)

But there have been times when the powers that be at the Academy did issue actual guidelines as to what the stars should wear. The first time this happened was in the lead-up to the 1942 ceremony, celebrating the films of the previous year. World War II was raging, and whether or not the Oscars should even be held was a source of controversy. At the end of 1941, Bette Davis was elected the president of the Academy and proposed a solution to the conundrum: The show should go on, but in a different format. Davis had a plan to do away with the dinner and dancing and switch the location to a theater where attendance would cost a $25 fee, which would be donated to war relief efforts. She was shot down and ultimately resigned from her post only a month after her election. The official line was "ill health," but Louella Parsons set out to tell the truth in what was likely a well-plotted PR stunt as well. Davis resigned because she felt that canceling the Oscars was a mistake.

The Board of Governors eventually came around to Davis's idea, and less than a month before the event, *Variety* ran a story detailing how the dinner would be held but would "nix finery, hoofing and glitter." The story explained: "Black ties and decollate will be strictly tabu, with business suits and infor- mal femme garb, obligatory." According to the official Acad- emy memo, reprinted in *Made for Each Other: Fashion and the Academy Awards*: "White tie, tuxedos and décolletage . . . very definitely out." Conservative gossip columnist Hedda Hopper was reportedly outraged by the decision, arguing that it would actually be inspiring to the troops to see famous people all decked out, but she was overruled. The Best Actress winner that year, Joan Fontaine, who won for Alfred Hitchcock's *Sus-*

picion, wore a black lace veil on her head and looked almost mournful when accepting her trophy. (The biggest legacy of the night was actually about the rivalry between her and her sister Olivia de Havilland, who was competing in the same category. Their hatred of one another is the stuff of legend.)

After the war there was a return to glamour, to such an extent that in 1952 the famed costume designer Edith Head, recipient of 19 consecutive nominations, was named "fashion consultant." Head described her role in 1966—the first year the awards were televised in color—as "really a referee." The idea was that Head would oversee what everyone was wearing so that nothing clashed. She advised against wearing red because it looked muddied on early TV feeds. In 1968 she sent out a memo about the "style of dress expected on stage." Per Head: "Actresses are requested to wear formal evening gowns either Maxi or floor length, preferably pastel shades since the setting is very formal and done entirely in white and gold. As you know, long dresses (no Mini or day length) are more graceful on stage and on camera in this type of background." Men were "expected to wear white tie with conventional formal evening accessories."

The memo was pointed. The year prior, Julie Christie, herself the victor for Best Actress at the 1966 ceremony, showed up to hand out Best Actor in a flouncy miniskirt. The thigh-forward cut was a signature of Christie's, but her choice, which clashed with Head's mandates for presenters, was derided. Hearst columnist Dorothy Manners wrote that Christie's "hideous miniskirt was nothing short of sheer insolence." The frenzy over the little dress, which, sure, made it look like she had walked off the set of *Laugh-In*, was apparently so intense that the movie for which she won, *Darling*, was rereleased to capitalize on the publicity.

Head's "mandates" were really strongly worded suggestions. They couldn't actually stop the participants from wearing whatever they wanted. (In 1969 Barbra Streisand wore a see-through pantsuit, after all . . .) After 1970, Head stepped down from the post. Her decrees may have been gone but her traditions were established. Rarely do Oscar dress codes make news these days, except when someone breaks the unspoken rules, or, of course, in the event of a pandemic.

The 2021 "Pandemic Oscars," held as countries were reeling from COVID-19, provided another occasion for those in charge to make some proclamations about what guests should and shouldn't wear. In a letter sent to nominees before the ceremony, the producers made some rules of their own: Zoom would not be permitted, nor would casual clothes. "You're wondering about the Dress Code (as well you should)," the decidedly quirky letter reads. "We're aiming for a fusion of Inspirational and Aspirational, which in actual words means formal is totally cool if you want to go there, but casual is really not." At the Golden Globes that year the at-home fashion ran the gamut from fashion pajamas to couture to hoodies. But the Oscars wanted none of that flippancy. Sure, they encouraged creativity, but not slovenliness.

Even amid unforeseen world events, the Oscars have standards, no matter how ridiculous they may sound. The 2021 producers' request for "aspirational" style is reminiscent of Hopper's complaints that the WWII Oscars would be too drab and Head's notion that the stars should match the aesthetic of the space. There may not be an official dress code, but the plebes watching from home should be impressed with whatever they see.

joan crawford

(1946)

I T'S ALMOST TOO EASY TO VIEW JOAN CRAWFORD accepting her Oscar for 1945's *Mildred Pierce* in bed as the height of diva behavior. It fits with everything we know about Crawford. Her legacy—as defined by the likes of *Mommie Dearest* and more recently Ryan Murphy's miniseries *Feud*—is that of a woman fueled by her jealousy, prone to wielding wire hangers like weapons. But was she unfairly maligned? Or truly as conniving as her reputation suggests? The truth was probably somewhere in between.

Despite allegedly being too sick to attend the Oscars ceremony, Crawford doesn't look very ill in the photos of her holding her trophy, awarded for playing a housewife attempting to provide the best life possible for her ungrateful teenage daughter. She smiles proudly from her alleged convalescence, wearing a full face of makeup. The existing photos are largely in black and white, but her garment was described in the press

as a "fluffy blue nightgown and coffee colored negligee." According to Patty Fox's book *Star Style*, the peignoir wasn't something she just had in her closet. It was designed by Helen Rose, the in-house costume designer for MGM, the studio where she had gotten her start. Fox writes that despite Crawford's surprise at winning, she and publicist Henry Rogers had campaigned heavily. The sickness could very well have been a publicity stunt. The pictures of Crawford in bed were just too ridiculous for newspapers not to run as the main illustration accompanying any story about the awards.

As Crawford tells it in her wonderfully titled book *A Portrait of Joan: The Autobiography of Joan Crawford*, she had been battling a flu on the set of her upcoming film *Humoresque*, which was under a strict production schedule. "Flu coupled with the nervous tension of being eligible for an Oscar had me shaking with chills and a fever," she wrote. "Although I was dressed to go, Dr. Bill Branch stepped in. 'Over my dead body,' he said. He put me back in bed and sat there to make sure I stayed." Photographers were also called to her house. Just in case she won, of course.

Still, the gossip goes that Crawford had another reason for staying home that night: She was certain that Ingrid Bergman was going to win for *The Bells of St. Mary's*, so she decided just to skip the party. Crawford played up how unexpected her win was in the press, telling the reporters gathered in her living room, "I voted for Bergman myself." (That seems doubtful, but it's a good soundbite.)

Crawford, maybe more than anyone in her category that night, needed this Oscar. As one headline blared, she had been trying to reach that kind of achievement for 21 years. She had been under contract with MGM since 1925, and by the 1940s her career was floundering. Making Warner Brothers' *Mildred Pierce* meant taking on a role that was outside her wheelhouse. Crawford was known for her sex appeal; yet in *Mildred Pierce* she played a working-class woman, beaten down by bad men and a worse teenager. She was attentive to how clothes would shape the character, buying housedresses from Sears Roebuck all on her own—though director Michael Curtiz didn't seem to realize the lengths to which she had gone, assuming she was wearing her signature shoulder pads even though she wasn't. Through this part, Crawford was deliberately trying to cast off her reputation as a fading star who only played ruthless women, like her role as an adulterer in *The Women*. "I sailed into Mildred with all the gusto I'd been saving for three years, not a Crawford mannerism, not a trace of my own personality," she wrote.

But her own personality ended up dominating her performance on Oscar night. No matter how much she tried to shed the glamour girl image in her role, as she sat in bed in that over-the-top nightgown, the fabric billowing around her, she was Joan Crawford, the movie star, with all of the peccadillos associated with that. Just a week later, her third divorce would make front-page news.

If her sickness was just a publicity stunt, then it was perhaps an ill-advised one. History would not remember those photos as the humbled star accepting her Oscar under duress. It would be another example of Joan Crawford, the diva, too embittered to get out of bed.

audrey hepburn

(1954)

WHEN AUDREY HEPBURN CAME TO COLLECT HER Oscar for 1953's *Roman Holiday*, she kept her eyes cast downward, her exaggerated lashes fluttering on her cheeks, as she slowly but deliberately said her thanks. Her reluctance to make eye contact with anyone in the crowd or play to the camera drew audiences' eyes to the neckline of her dress. The lace fabric swept across her collarbone in a straight line in a way that was at once demure, coated in lace, and thoroughly modern—for the era—with seams tapered to show off her shoulders.

The Academy proves time and time again that it loves an ingenue—from Katharine Hepburn's first win for *Morning Glory* to Jennifer Lawrence's for *Silver Linings Playbook*. But there has never been anyone that's more of an ingenue than Audrey Hepburn in *Roman Holiday*. She wasn't predicted to win, according to her biographer Barry Paris. The favorite was

Deborah Kerr, rolling in the sand in *From Here to Eternity*. But Audrey was immediately a princess—that's what she played in *Roman Holiday*, after all—and she needed a crown. Behind the scenes she was not the naïf she may have appeared to be, but a woman carefully wielding her newfound influence.

By the time *Roman Holiday* was released, Hepburn was already being spoken about in extraordinary terms. An article about her love life in *Screenland* notes that she "has been described as 'romantic; fey; puckish; whimsical; demure; mischievous; pert; naive; passionate; captivating; beguiling; sensitive.'" It gushes that she's "gifted with a long-legged grace, a mobile face with big, slated dark eyes, and a rich, slightly clotted voice."

Roman Holiday helped her emerge fully formed as a style icon. Her aesthetic was as crucial to her portrayal of the rebellious Princess Ann as her aching, lovelorn acting. Ann undergoes a transformation over the course of William Wyler's film. One of the first things she does after escaping her royal trappings is restyle herself. She ditches the puffy, prim sleeves on her blouse and unbuttons her collar. She cuts her long hair into a gamine pixie. The hairdresser, hitting on her, asks, "You musician maybe? You artist? Painter?" She shakes her head. "I know," he declares. "You, model." Her new look, scarf around her neck, was simultaneously boyish, sexy, and ultrafeminine.

It emphasizes her tiny waist, which years from then would be used as "thinspiration" on the internet, an unobtainable goal for many struggling with body image.

The tea-length garment Hepburn chose for the Academy Awards somehow falls in between Ann's casual ensemble and the more ornate royal gowns on display. It's sprightly but appears delicate, like it would shatter if you touched it. The dress's origin story is messy. It's widely considered the first time the actress appeared publicly in a piece designed by Hubert de Givenchy, and certainly, it looks like something Givenchy would have made. But Kerry Taylor, who sold the dress through her eponymous auction house in 2011, tells a different story. "It is definitely not by Givenchy," she wrote in an email to me in 2018, when this essay was originally published in Medium. "It was a dress designed for the film by Edith Head, which Audrey had remodeled for the Oscar ceremony—a 'make do and mend' mentality that she had inherited from those years of hardship during the war." Hepburn, daughter of a Dutch baroness, lived in the Netherlands during World War II. She was malnourished—often one of the reasons cited for her skinniness, which was envied by many in a sort of perverse adoration—and she volunteered with the resistance, performing in underground ballet recitals to raise money for people being persecuted by the Nazis. She was so young as an Oscar nominee, but had already defined herself once before and possessed an industrial spirit from her early hardships.

As Taylor further explained to me, Audrey removed the stately suited bodice that appeared on the gown in the film's final scene and added the Givenchy-influenced boatneck. Regardless of who was responsible—Givenchy or Head—what was perfectly clear at the ceremony was that Audrey herself was taking control of her look.

In the lead-up to Oscar night, a conflict between Head and Givenchy unfolded behind the scenes on *Sabrina*, Audrey's *Roman Holiday* follow-up. By all accounts, Audrey was playing puppet master. Head, the costume supervisor for Paramount, was reportedly eager to tackle the project, writing in her memoir that she considered the romantic comedy a "perfect setup" for her work. Various sources tell the story in slightly different ways, but the crux of it was that Audrey, dissatisfied with Head's solo work, implored director Billy Wilder to let her go to Paris and woo Givenchy.

In *Made for Each Other: Fashion and the Academy Awards*, Bronwyn Cosgrave writes that Audrey "went above Head" by arguing that it made sense for her titular character to return from Paris, where she is sent after a suicide attempt, with a wardrobe of couture. (Givenchy, meanwhile, only first entertained meeting the young actress in his studio because he thought she was Katharine Hepburn.) Despite Givenchy's skepticism of the confident unknown, Audrey was persistent. "I told Audrey that I had very few workers and I needed all my hands to help me with my next collection, which I had to show very soon. But she insisted, 'Please, please, there must be something I can try on,'" he once reminisced in an interview with *Vanity Fair*. The Givenchy version of events found Hepburn selecting items from the spring/summer 1953 collection, among them a black number with a neckline that echoes the one on the Oscar dress. She liked it, per *VF*, because of how it highlighted qualities on her body she thought were assets (her shoulders) and concealed what, in her opinion, was not (her, in the words of Givenchy himself, "skinny collarbone").

Both Head and Givenchy had misgivings about the way they were treated on *Sabrina*. In a 2010 *Los Angeles Times* piece excerpted from the memoir of Jean-Pierre Dorléac, Head maintained that she was responsible for the costumes. Meanwhile, Givenchy was frustrated to find his name excised from the movie's credits. But the history books, however, give Givenchy victory over Head in the Audrey business. The designer's name became linked with Audrey's, even inspiring tomes about their collaboration. Givenchy went on to design more memorable looks for her in *Funny Face* and the dorm-room staple of her pictures: *Breakfast at Tiffany's*. He'd even get credit for the Oscar dress. When Emma Stone accepted her award in Givenchy, the brand confirmed that she was the first Best Actress to do so since Audrey. The breathless desire to link Emma to Audrey only goes to show how much influence the latter still holds over what we consider glamorous.

But really, this all just proved Audrey's savviness. By enlisting Givenchy—even if it was at the expense of Head, who did her part to cultivate the Hepburn milieu—she embraced the identity of fashion icon that would leave a lasting mark on the red carpet. She seems almost meek on that stage accepting her trophy. When she first climbs the stairs, she even walks in the wrong direction. She may have been an ingenue, but Audrey was just beginning her reign.

miyoshi umeki

(1958)

"WHAT A CUTE THING SHE WAS IN HER NATIVE costume." That's what Louella Parsons wrote after Miyoshi Umeki became the first person of Asian descent to win an Oscar for her role in the 1957 film *Sayonara*. Umeki wore a kimono to the ceremony in March of 1958. There aren't many color photos of the garment remaining. It was dark, with a detailed floral design around the bottom half. The obi—the sash around her waist—was emblazoned with a gold accent. When her name was called by Anthony Quinn, Umeki made her way up to the stage, a big smile on her face. She bowed to him before accepting the trophy. "I really don't know what to say," she said at the podium. "I wish somebody were to help me right now, 'cause I didn't expect so I had nothing in my mind. But right now I thank you for everyone who help me, and you, and you, and all American people."

To this day, only three performers of East Asian descent have won Oscars: Umeki, Haing S. Ngor, who won for the 1984 film *The Killing Fields,* and Yuh-Jung Youn for *Minari* in 2021. Umeki was a pioneer, even if her contributions to the industry have been largely forgotten. From what is known, it would appear that she wanted to forget the industry as well. She retired from acting in 1972, after her television series *The Courtship of Eddie's Father* was canceled. According to an *Entertainment Weekly* report in 2018, she threw away her Oscar, scratching out her name before getting rid of it. Umeki clearly wanted to leave this world behind, and it's easy to see why: Even in the triumph of her Oscar win, her accomplishment was diminished. It's there in Parsons's words. The famed columnist didn't marvel at Umeki's gorgeous kimono. She didn't take into account the pride with which Umeki might have worn it. Instead she use racially charged language to deem the actress just a "cute thing" in a "native costume" and "a lovely little bit of Japanese porcelain."

The 1958 Oscars should be regarded in many ways as a landmark year for actors from Japan. Not only did Umeki win, but her countryman Sessue Hayakawa also became the first Asian person ever nominated for Best Supporting Actor, playing the cruel Colonel Saito in the Best Picture winner, *The Bridge on the River Kwai*. Both *Bridge* and *Sayonara* offered new levels of exposure for Japanese actors but were equally laden with stereotypes. While *Bridge* reignites the notion of the Japanese as villains, *Sayonara* is a plea for racial harmony, which nonetheless relies on the inaccurate and harmful notion of Asian women as subservient and exotic. Keep in mind that less than 20 years earlier, the U.S. had interned Japanese Americans in one of the greatest violations of human rights in the country's history. Nearly 70 years later, six Asian women would be massacred in a series of shootings at Georgia spas.

Joshua Logan's *Sayonara*, based on a novel by James Michener, centers on Army Major Lloyd Gruver. After serving in the Korean War, Gruver, played by Marlon Brando, is reassigned to Japan, where a member of his unit, Joe Kelly (Red Buttons), is set to marry a Japanese woman, Katsumi (Umeki). Gruver is initially critical of Kelly's union, calling Katsumi a "slant-eyed runt," but upon arriving in the country he finds himself falling in love with a Japanese woman himself, Hana-ogi (Miiko Taka), a star of an all-female revue. Umeki portrays Katsumi as gentle and soft-spoken, with a limited understanding of English. She serves the American men around her silently. In one scene she's seen bathing Joe. We're meant to believe that the love between Katsumi and Joe is true, but she is never developed as a character beyond her relationship to her husband. The only moment where the audience gets a taste of what she might be feeling is toward the end of the film, when Joe discovers that she was planning on getting a surgery to create a fold in her upper eyelid so she could "pass" as a white, American woman. Joe throws her to the ground, angry that she could consider such an alteration. It's the moment in the film that these days you would call the "Oscar clip"—the big moment of dramatic acting that would get played during the telecast. But it's also distressing to see Katsumi brutalized, even and perhaps especially by someone who loves her. While Lloyd and Hana-ogi get a happy ending, Joe and Katsumi do not. Facing the risk of being separated by the U.S. Army, they die in each other's arms in what is implied to be a consensual murder-suicide. What was positioned as romantic now seems eerie: a white man killing himself and his lover to evade separation.

Umeki was born in Hokkaido and began her career as a singer, memorizing jazz songs in order to learn English and performing for American GIs near her home. According to a syndicated news story from after her win, she was performing at a club in the San Fernando Valley when she was spotted by an executive, which led to her casting in *Sayonara*. Her obituary in the *Guardian* tells it slightly differently: She appeared on a variety show called *Arthur Godfrey and His Friends*, which caught the eye of a Warner Brothers casting agent.

Umeki never explained if she chose to wear a kimono as a point of national pride or a matter of comfort. But for a young woman who grew up obsessing over American entertainment, she herself was defined by the limited American ideas of her nationality, even when she defied them. That syndicated story describes her in contradictory terms. She takes a "drag of a cigarette" but is a "button-eyed doll" wearing a kimono. The same article ran with different headlines in different papers. The *Post-Crescent* from Appleton, Wisconsin, labeled it: "American Success Story Told by Miyoshi Umeki, Oscar Winner." The *Marshfield News-Herald*, also from Wisconsin, framed it as "Jap Winner of Oscar Is Elated," using a racial slur to describe Umeki.

Parsons caught up with Umeki later that year, when she was about to star in the Broadway production of *Flower Drum Song*, the Rodgers and Hammerstein musical, which would later be adapted into a film, also starring Umeki. Umeki was confident, telling Parsons: "How can you lose with Rodgers and Hammerstein? The show is already sold out until spring. I'm sleeping well these nights." Parsons appeared to be taken aback by Umeki's boldness. "Even when Miyoshi was in Hollywood, I failed to detect an overabundance of 'typical' Japanese humility in her makeup," Parsons wrote. Parsons, and probably so many others, saw a woman in a kimono bow as she received her Oscar and made the racist assumption that Umeki was demure. And while Umeki's legacy may be clouded with various mysteries, there was no mistaking her for a shrinking violet.

JOANNE WOODWARD

(1958)

THE SAME YEAR MIYOSHI UMEKI CAME TO THE OSCARS at the Pantages Theatre wearing a kimono, another winner decided on a similarly personally evocative choice of attire. Joanne Woodward, who took home Best Actress for *The Three Faces of Eve*, attended in an emerald green dress she had made herself. It was sleeveless, with a full skirt, and she accessorized with white gloves. If Woodward hadn't said that she sewed it herself from a mere $125 worth of fabric, it might have been hard to tell it was handmade. Perhaps if you looked closely you would notice that the tailoring is lacking some of the sleekness that one expects at the Oscars, but it's still gorgeous in glistening green.

It's hard to picture any other star taking to her needle for Oscar night of all nights, but Woodward remains one of the most down-to-earth figures to ever grace the industry, even as she was part of one of the most talked about relationships in Hollywood history.

Why did Woodward make her dress herself? Like a number of other women featured here, she was guided by low expectations. "I didn't think I had a chance," she told the Associated Press. "So I didn't want to invest too much." Despite her modesty, Woodward gave the kind of performance the

Oscars tend to love. In *The Three Faces of Eve* she plays a woman with multiple personalities: There's meek housewife Eve White, the salacious Eve Black, and then, finally, a neutral presence known as Jane. The film is proud of its based-on-a-true-story credentials. It's narrated by the journalist Alistair Cooke, who assured the audience that what they are in fact seeing is fact.

Woodward was still a fairly new face when she beat out the likes of Deborah Kerr and Elizabeth Taylor, but she had been struggling to make her way in the business for years. She had a contract at 20th Century Fox but had only made two films, after which she moved back to New York, where she had previously studied, to do a play. Some years earlier she was understudying on Broadway in William Inge's *Picnic* where she met the man she would eventually marry the same year she won her Oscar: Paul Newman.

Though Newman was nowhere near as famous as he would eventually become, being part of a celebrity couple was part of the allure that drew the press to Woodward following her Oscar win. Their film *The Long, Hot Summer*, based on William Faulkner stories, was just about to be released. In the sweaty romantic picture, directed by Martin Ritt, he plays an interloper who tries his best to woo the town schoolteacher, played by Woodward, eventually succeeding.

Despite their beauty and their fame, there was something thoroughly relatable about this couple. After Woodward won her Oscar, Newman reportedly didn't want to take photos with her so as not to hog her spotlight. According to *Motion Picture Daily*, he "kept insisting" it was "her night." The *Detroit Free-Press* wrote a profile of Woodward highlighting her humble beginnings and perseverance, noting how just a year before her Oscar win she was eating corned beef hash for Thanksgiving dinner.

The fact that she had sewn her own dress only added to the conception that she was somehow more regular than other stars. When a museum in her home state of Georgia wanted to put it on display, she declined the offer. "I spent nearly $100 for the material, designed the dress, and worked on it for three weeks," she said, according to the *Pomona Progress Bulletin*. "Why, I'm almost as proud of the dress as I am of the Oscar."

She even considered wearing it again. "I thought I would wear it again the other night, but I just couldn't," she dished to columnist Erskine Johnson. "It's now packed away with my wedding gown."

Woodward would continue to be the rare, wholesome, quote-unquote real celebrity. She and Newman remained married until his death in 2008, a long-lasting couple in a business where divorce feels like the norm. They lived away from Hollywood in Westport, Connecticut, eschewing the spotlight. In the late 1980s, Woodward went to college, getting her degree from Sarah Lawrence at the same time her daughter did. The Newman Foundation created a public policy chair in her name, according to the *New York Times*, "encouraging undergraduates to seek careers in public service."

And it all makes perfect sense for the young woman who, faced with one of the biggest nights of her career, decided to sit down and sew. Just as she and Newman made a life for themselves away from the gleam of Hollywood excess, she made a dress for herself that maybe wasn't the couture her cohorts were wearing, but was meaningful all on its own.

rita moreno

(1962)

R ITA MORENO CAME TO THE 2018 OSCARS WIELDING the ultimate flex. She appeared in a 56-year-old dress— but not just any 56-year-old dress. It was the very same dress she wore in 1962 when she claimed her Supporting Actress trophy for playing Anita in *West Side Story*. She made a couple of amendments to the gown for its second outing. She got rid of the bateau neckline in favor of a strapless look. She added some regal accessories: a gold cuff around her neck and a black headband crowning her cropped cut, now gray. And aside from a few wrinkles and the addition of glasses, she looked largely the same, an ageless wonder with the same spirit and, if we're being real, the same banging bod. She won unanimous praise from the press, fashion and otherwise. "Rita Moreno is honestly an inspiration to us all," *Cosmopolitan* hailed. The *New York Times* declared that "recycling has never been more elegant."

Showing the world that you can still rock an iconic dress more than half a century later is certainly reason enough to wear it, but Moreno's choice also spoke volumes about an industry that provides few opportunities for Latinx performers. For Moreno, physically, it was a blessing that not much had changed, but symbolically it was evidence of a world stuck in the past.

Moreno—as she told Ryan Seacrest on the 2018 red carpet, after making fun of him for reading off a teleprompter—was not expecting to win that night in 1962. She was up against Judy Garland, who was moving away from her reputation as Dorothy with an acclaimed serious turn in *Judgment at Nuremberg*. Still, Moreno decided to fly in from the Philippines, where she was shooting the B-movie *Cry of Battle*, just in case. She was allowed only three days off to attend the ceremony and acquired her dress before departing for the U.S. "I ordered a heavily brocaded dress made of special Japanese obi fabric, a gorgeous gown with a black bateau top that I still have (and can get into happily)," she wrote in her 2013 memoir, foreshadowing the moment she would step into it again.

Breaking into Hollywood was not easy for Moreno, who would eventually go on to complete her EGOT (Emmy, Grammy, Oscar, Tony), becoming one of the rare performers to win all the major performing arts trophies. Even prior to gaining widespread fame with *West Side Story*, the Puerto Rican Moreno was speaking out about the lack of opportunities for Latinx actors. She developed a reputation for refusing to remain quiet. Speaking with the Associated Press in 1960, Moreno asked, "Why oh why do Latin girls on the screen always have to be tempestuous sexpots? It's a stereotype. It's also stupid. Is every Latin woman a sexpot? Of course not. They're just the same as other women." In November 1961, the month after *West Side Story* premiered, *Holiday Magazine* labeled her "Hollywood's most outspoken actress," writing that "the studio brass regards her as 'stubborn,' 'uncooperative,' and 'opinionated.'" She was not cheered for highlighting injustices. Rather, she was deemed a problem. She forged ahead.

Anita was different from the roles she had been offered before. "This is the first time I've played a real woman," she told the AP. "At this point, I had never been given the opportunity to play the part of a woman who stood up for herself," she wrote in her memoir. "Her suffering, her anger, were my suffering, my anger." But Moreno was also keenly aware of how the film was perpetrating cultural inaccuracies: She was frustrated that all the actors playing the Puerto Rican gang the Sharks were made to wear makeup to look the same shade of brown, and how white actress Natalie Wood, as the heroine Maria, was "uncomfortable" around the dancers. And though Moreno brought her own experiences and pain to Anita—especially in the scene where she is cruelly harassed and nearly raped by members of the Jets—she saw herself reduced in a *New York Times* review to her "least favorite cliché: 'Spitfire.'"

As she was winning great critical acclaim, her personal life was spiraling. Her ongoing affair with Marlon Brando was taking a toll both emotionally and physically. When she became pregnant, the actor forced Moreno to undergo an abortion, and the doctor botched the procedure. Instead of being concerned with Moreno's well-being, Brando just thought he got ripped off. "Afterward, I had a hollow feeling and couldn't control my emotions," she explained. When Brando became romantically involved with another woman, Moreno fell deeper into a depression that was augmented by the phenobarbital she was taking to deal with a thyroid condition. One morning, after Brando had left, she took sleeping pills in his apartment. "This wasn't a revenge suicide, but a consolation, an escape-from-pain death."

Taking on the *Cry of Battle* role was part of Moreno's plan to forge ahead following her suicide attempt. It was a "paycheck," she wrote, but she felt some solace being in a place "nearly identical to the rain forest of [her] childhood, El Yunque." Hollywood and success called her back with her nomination.

Moreno was so surprised when her name was called by Rock Hudson on Oscar night that "Hollywood's most outspoken actress" was rendered speechless. She hugged her costar George Chakiris and ran up to collect her prize. "I can't believe it," she sighed. "Good lord. I leave you with that." And then she hustled off the stage. She knew her win was more than just a personal triumph. She wrote that her friend told her how her victory was celebrated in New York's Puerto Rican neighborhoods. "People were literally hanging out their windows, yelling, 'She won! She won! She did it!' What they were really saying was, 'We won!'" The *New York Herald Tribune* said she looked "resplendent" in her gown.

Moreno was under the impression that this would change everything for her. "My career was certainly on the wane," she told the *Los Angeles Times*. "And, suddenly, with one film, to have all this happen!" But that gold man did not portend the wealth of roles for which Moreno was hoping. Instead, her career stalled. After *Cry of Battle* came out in 1963, she didn't make another movie for six years. In 1964, the *New York World-Telegram* ran a story with the headline "Oscar No Aid to Rita Moreno." In it, she declared, "The power of the Academy Award is a myth." Though she had been given acting's highest accolade, producers still saw Moreno as, in her words, the "barefoot girl."

As of publication, Moreno is one of only four Latinx performers to win a trophy for acting. In 2018, the same year that Moreno revived her dress, Laura Bradley at *Vanity Fair* wrote that the event was "a celebration of Latinx talent—with no Latinx acting nominees." Even with Mexican director Guillermo Del Toro winning Best Director and Best Picture for *The Shape of Water*, it seemed frustratingly like Hollywood was praising only a certain type of Latinx contribution. "One interesting observation in the Academy landscape is a larger tally of Latinx in categories like production design," Clayton Davis wrote in *Variety* in 2020. "Six winners in 18 individual nominations are a much better showing than the others previously mentioned. Which begs the question, 'why are we good enough to build your sets, but not good enough to be in front of your cameras?'"

When Moreno stepped back into that shimmering skirt, it felt as if she was referencing both her own staying power and how little had changed for performers like her in the intervening decades. For as beloved as she is, she could have done so much more if she weren't trapped in a system that locked her into stereotypes and punished her self-advocacy. It's a cycle that has repeated itself. Her beloved television show *One Day at a Time* had to continually fight for renewal on two different platforms before ultimately being canceled in 2020.

She walked out on that Dolby stage in 2018 facing a new, more diverse Academy, one that, hopefully, appreciated the wealth of her talents even as it remained stuck in some of its most frustrating ways. Moreno struck a pose before presenting the award for Best Foreign Language Film, highlighting her gown's eccentric silhouette, with its wide hips and golden pattern. It was as if to say, *"Hey, guys, remember me?"*

barbra streisand

(1969)

ARBRA STREISAND FIGURED THAT HER FIRST TIME being nominated for an Oscar would not be her last. That was among the reasons she chose to wear her now infamous Arnold Scaasi glittery pantsuit to the Dorothy Chandler Pavilion in 1969. She would later reminisce: "I wanted a white collar and cuffs, which it had, and I wore my hair under my chin, because I thought to myself, I'm going to win two Oscars in my lifetime, and I'll be more conservative next time." Of course, Babs was saying this with the benefit of hindsight. She gave the quote to *W* in 2012, after she had already collected both of her trophies. Still, Barbra had earned that bombast even back in 1969.

When the multitalented icon won her first Oscar for her performance as vaudevillian Fanny Brice, it was the anointing of a woman who was already a sensation. It also marked a moment of transition between Old and New Hollywood, both spiritually and visually. Over the years Barbra's outfit, which was unintentionally see-through, has been derided as a fashion misstep, but it's also the mark of a 27-year-old embracing her youth just as her legend is being crystallized.

She may not have yet hit 30, but Barbra was already *Barbra* when she was up for Best Actress for *Funny Girl*, William Wyler's movie adaptation of the Broadway musical that made her a star. Her rise had been documented on the covers of major magazines. She was the kid from Flatbush, with *that* nose, who had defied the powers that be who called her ugly with her incredible talent. She was frequently defined by what her looks were not. In the story that accompanied her cover of *Life* in 1964, when *Funny Girl* was running on Broadway, Shana Alexander wrote: "When, five years ago, 16-year-old Barbra decided to leave Flatbush, invade Broadway, and aim for the stars, she had every mark of a loser. She was homely, kooky, friendless, scared, and broke. She had a big nose, skinny legs, no boyfriends, a conviction that she was about to die from a mysterious disease, no place to sleep but a portable folding cot and, worst of all, a supersensitive brain which could exquisitely comprehend precisely how much of a loser she actually was." In a *Time* article the same year—she was also on the cover—she was described as a "carelessly stacked girl with long nose and bones awry." The implication in all these pieces is that Streisand entered the stratosphere in spite of the way she looked.

By the time her Fanny Brice was immortalized on-screen she was already a best-selling recording artist and a Tony nominee twice over. She was also, somewhat controversially, a member of the Academy, even though you typically have to have worked on a movie to be admitted. The film version of *Funny Girl*, as Renata Adler wrote in the *New York Times*, was designed to propel her to a new level of stardom. Adler's review is dismissive of basically the whole enterprise, save for Barbra. "When she is singing—in a marvelous scene on roller skates—when she throws a line away, or shrugs, or looks funny or sad, she has a power, gentleness, and intensity that rather knocks all the props and sets and camera angles on their ear," Adler wrote. (Adler remained frustrated at what she saw as the film's condescension toward Barbra's appearance: "as though there were some special virtue in making a movie star out of someone who is not likely to be whistled at on Main Street or featured in cold-cream commercials.")

It's not like Barbra actually needed to win an Oscar to achieve the status she now holds. So perhaps that was what she was thinking when she decided she would have some fun with her outfit. As Scaasi, a designer who was on the rise at the time, recalled in the *Los Angeles Times*, he told Streisand: "Let's show people how young and cute you are. Let's forget that elegant bit." Streisand remembered having two options. One "lovely, but very conservative" and the other was "the pantsuit with plastic sequins." She went for the pantsuit.

The Scaasi is an exercise in 1960s camp. Part Wednesday Addams, part Studio 54, both the top and the bottoms flare out to create the sensation that the ensemble is quite literally swinging back and forth. Barbra wore her hair in a bouffant, with her signature long nails and cat eye. She looks like she wandered out of Andy Warhol's Factory and into the Dorothy Chandler. Frankly, I've never understood the disdain, which came instantly. Writing in the *Hollywood Citizen*, columnist Belle Greenberg declared that her "see-through thing was yeuch." But to the modern eye Barbra looks cool and sexy. Streisand herself maintains that she wasn't aware that the whole thing was transparent. She's never seemed too bothered about it, though. In the lights, yes, you could see the outline of her bum, but it was somehow still almost bashful while also being revealing.

Barbra's win marked one of the rare times in Oscar history that voting actually resulted in a tie. The first name that was called was Katharine Hepburn's. The revered actress—herself never one to shy away from a bold pants moment—wasn't in attendance. Her proxy escorted Streisand to the stage. Streisand had to remove her gum before standing up and adjusting her pants as she made her way to collect her prize. Climbing up the stage, she tripped over one of the protruding, extravagant bell-bottoms. It was a moment that felt, well, a little Fanny Brice—unintentionally goofy, but easily brushed off. The double win felt like a changing of the guard. Out with one icon and in with another. Barbra had plenty of experiences like that in her nascent career. She was anointed by Judy Garland in 1963, when she was 21 and they sang a duet on Garland's TV show. Even playing Fanny Brice connected Barbra to the legacy of another great brash lady with a gift for performing. But when she accepted her Oscar in Scaasi's bold creation, she broke free from all of her antecedents and started a reign all on her own—with a little hint of ass.

JENNIFER LAWRENCE

(2013)

BARBRA STREISAND WAS NOT THE ONLY PERSON TO TRIP on a complicated garment on the way to collect her Best Actress trophy. More recently, and possibly more infamously, Jennifer Lawrence took a tumble on her massive Dior gown when coming up to accept the award for *Silver Linings Playbook*. Whereas Barbra sort of daintily stumbled over her Scaasi pants, Lawrence ended up on the floor, in a mass of billowing champagne pink fabric.

It was the cap on Lawrence's run of being a Hashtag Relatable Queen on her way to get the little gold man. As her fellow winner for Best Supporting Actress Anne Hathaway was being derided for being too desperate, Lawrence was being praised for being quote-unquote fun and chill, even on the highest stages. The dichotomy crystallized when their names were called. Hathaway, perfectly rehearsed, said, "It came true." Lawrence, having just crowed about wanting

McDonald's on the red carpet, fell over her gown. She got a standing ovation. "You guys are just standing up because you feel bad that I fell and that's really embarrassing," she said in response.

But it's not as if her image hadn't been as carefully constructed—if not even more so—than Hathaway's. Lawrence became a renowned actress after starring in, and getting her first Oscar nomination for, Debra Granik's 2010 film *Winter's Bone*. She was then plucked to anchor the massive *Hunger Games* franchise around the same time she hitched her wagon to director David O. Russell, who cast her to play the volatile lead in *Silver Linings Playbook*, a rom-com about mental illness and a dance competition.

By the time the awards season celebrating the movies of 2012 rolled around, Lawrence had signed a contract with Dior. Even as she claimed not to care about fashion, she was being anointed by one of the most revered houses. At each ceremony that awards season, Lawrence arrived in a different Dior gown. When she claimed her Golden Globe, it was an orange-red belted number. Holding her SAG Award, it was formfitting and sleeveless and blue. In the lead-up to the big day, Lawrence joked that she was going to wear "sweatpants," before explaining that she actually was going to go even more formal than her first trip to the ceremony, saying she'd had a change of heart:

"That's the problem with the Oscars: They're always at the end where you are just exhausted from dressing up, so I never care. Now, I will. Fashion."

This Dior looked almost bridal, with a prodigious skirt clustering around her legs. It was also apparently very hard to walk in. Why did she fall? Well, she revealed that years later in classic Lawrence fashion: "I was at the Oscars, waiting to hear if my name was called, and I kept thinking, Cakewalk, cakewalk, cakewalk. I thought, Why is 'cakewalk' stuck in my head? And then, as I started to walk up the stairs and the fabric from my dress tucked under my feet, I realized my stylist had told me, 'Kick, walk, kick, walk.' You are supposed to kick the dress out while you walk, and I totally forgot because I was thinking about cake! And that's why I fell."

The fall was immediately branded as endearing—just another example of J. Law being J. Law. But there were some who side-eyed the trip as yet another carefully crafted bit of image-making, a theory that gained steam when Lawrence also ate shit the following year, collapsing on the red carpet. Both fans and formalwear can be fickle.

jane
fonda

(1972)

TWO YEARS BEFORE JANE FONDA WOULD WIN AN Oscar for her work playing call girl Bree Daniels in *Klute*, she received her first nomination for her role in the Depression-era saga *They Shoot Horses, Don't They?* She attended the awards, but felt somehow disconnected from them, she wrote in her memoir *My Life: So Far*. "That night felt different—not just because I was a nominee," she explained, "but because my life outside of movies was starting to interest me more than being an actor."

By the time she was nominated for *Klute*, Fonda's celebrity had morphed completely. While she was giving one of the best performances of her career, she was transforming herself into an activist. She hadn't yet made her controversial trip to North Vietnam, gaining the nickname "Hanoi Jane," but was already an antiwar activist targeted by J.

Edgar Hoover's FBI. She was arrested at Cleveland's Hopkins International Airport for drug possession after a speaking tour on college campuses. The "drugs" they found were her vitamins. Her mug shot became a sensation, both politically and aesthetically.

Fonda came to the Oscars not just as an actor being honored for her great work on film, but as the face of a movement. And she was in a precarious position. She wanted to use her platform but wished to do so wisely. Instead of the festive dress that women of her stature usually donned, she wore all black. With her hair still cut in the iconic shag from her mug shot, she turned to a black Yves Saint Laurent suit she had acquired in 1968, around the same time she was first experiencing her political awakening. "I wore something that made a statement," she would later tell the *New York Times*. "It was not a time for showy dresses. It was a time for seriousness."

Fonda, as she frequently said at the time, only became an activist in her 30s. "I'm 34, I didn't become active until I was 32 for God's sake," she explained to the *Los Angeles Times* in an article that ran a couple of months before the Oscars. She recognized how her late entry into political zealousness made some people skeptical of the work she was doing. Before shooting *Klute* she went on a trip across America, visiting the Paiute and Shoshone Native American reservations and engaging in what she calls her "first public act against the war," a two-day fast. She brought books to GIs, gave speeches, and handed out leaflets. She attended her first national antiwar rally. Her style was evolving too. She explained that she had decided to stop dressing for men's attention. The woman who was known across the world as Barbarella in the campy, borderline pornographic sci-fi classic directed by her then-husband ditched miniskirts. "My wardrobe was pared down to a few pairs of jeans, some drip-dry shirts, army boots, and a heavy navy pea jacket," she wrote.

Fonda threw herself into research for *Klute* with the same level of intensity, speaking with call girls and madams. She didn't think she was right for the part of Bree, even suggesting that Faye Dunaway take over, but director Alan J. Pakula wouldn't hear of it. She resolved to bring new depths to the kind of role that had so often been minimized. Her work paid off. Roger Ebert raved about her in his review of the film. "What is it about Jane Fonda that makes her such a fascinating actress to watch? She has a sort of nervous intensity that keeps her so firmly locked into a film character that the character actually seems distracted by things that come up in the movie," he wrote. "You almost have the feeling, a couple of times in *Klute*, that the Fonda character had other plans and was just leaving the room when this (whatever it is) came up." The great Pauline Kael declared that "there isn't another young dramatic actress in American films who can touch" her.

Fonda's portrayal of Bree still feels revolutionary all these years later. She's a sex worker who is not defined by her sex work. Her relationship to it is nuanced: She's troubled by her desire to always return to turning tricks, but she's not apologetic. She gets pleasure out of her job and the ways she can manipulate men, and she's also introspective about those traits.

For as creatively successful as the filming of *Klute* was, Fonda also recalls in her memoir that it was her first time wrestling with a new experience: "Being hated." The hostility she experienced on set—not from her costar Donald Sutherland or director Pakula—was subtle but pointed. She arrived one day to find an American flag hanging above the set of her character's apartment, taunting her with the notion that she was unpatriotic.

This idea that her politics could hurt her career would persist, but she plowed ahead. She and *Klute* costar Sutherland established the FTA, the Free Theater Associates also known as Free the Army, which performed as a sort of alternative USO show on military bases in the Pacific. Her nomination was used, in one report, as proof that the Academy was "not vindictive" toward someone as outspoken as she was. "Miss Fonda, always on the ramparts demeaning the establishment and the U.S. government, was nominated despite her unpopular stands," the story read. That's the kind of minefield Fonda was walking into at the Dorothy Chandler Pavilion.

Fonda wanted to make a statement, but she wasn't sure how she should go about it. One way would be with her clothing. The elegant but stark suit had a Maoist element to its collar, as the *New York Times* would note years later when discussing Fonda's influence as a fashion icon. She took the same approach to her speech as she did with her outfit: She would say a lot by saying very little at all. She asked her father, renowned actor Henry, how to proceed, and he suggested: "Tell 'em there's a lot to say, but tonight isn't the time." She took his advice. Upon taking her trophy from Walter Matthau, she was met with extended applause. According to a *Los Angeles Times* report, there were some boos, but you can't hear them in the footage that lives on. She took a few bows. Her speech was short. "There's a great deal to say and I'm not going to say it tonight, I would just like to thank you very much." She let her mourning attire do the work. Decades later, Fonda's choice of dress for the ceremony would be held up as an example for other women to follow at the 2018 Golden Globes, when the attending actresses decided to wear all black as a sign of solidarity with the #MeToo movement.

In the years that followed her win for *Klute*, Fonda never underestimated the power of a recognizable visual as a symbol for one's opinions. Well into her 80s, she would regain her political icon status by staging a series of protests known as Fire Drill Fridays outside of the Capitol to bring attention to the climate crisis. She was arrested frequently. Her attire? A bright red coat, which became her signature look, just like that black suit all those years before.

diana
ross

(1973)

DIANA ROSS PLANNED A COSTUME CHANGE MID-Oscars. She arrived at the Dorothy Chandler Pavilion in a spectacular three-piece suit, made of silver satin with bell-bottoms around the ankles. But if you watch footage of her category, Best Actress, being announced, you'll notice she's no longer in that adventurous take on menswear. She's in a black gown, with black fur around her shoulders. Why two different outfits?

Well, because she was Diana Ross, after all. "She was the only one that would do that," designer Bob Mackie, who was responsible for both of her ensembles, told me.

There aren't many photographs available of the black dress, but there were supposed to be. Ross, at least in her mind, was supposed to win. That second ensemble would have been the one she was photographed in holding her trophy, triumphant.

She would have been the first Black woman to ever win Best Actress, an achievement that wouldn't happen until Halle Berry did so in 2002 (see page 132). That dress would have been etched in history alongside Berry's floral Elie Saab.

But Ross didn't win. Liza Minnelli's name was called. Judy Garland's daughter ascended in a yellow Halston, while Ross masked her disappointment. That black dress is not remembered. But that suit is etched in the books of Oscar attire, one of the greats of music flexing her sartorial muscles as she enters the world of moviemaking.

Ross was a risky choice to play the role of Billie Holiday in *Lady Sings the Blues*, the biopic for which she was nominated. Even Berry Gordy, the founder of Motown who helped Ross rise to fame as a member of The Supremes, was skeptical—despite his own interest in establishing her as a movie star. According to J. Randy Taraborrelli's biography of the superstar, Gordy told producer Jay Weston, who was stuck on the idea of Ross in the role, that he wouldn't have Ross playing a "junkie." The record executive eventually came around and ended up putting the strength of his signature organization behind the film. But Ross had to convince more people than just Gordy that she was up to the challenge. The general sentiment prior to the release of *Lady Sings the Blues* was that Ross was a bad casting choice, a pop star attempting something beyond her depth. "My God what had I done to deserve this total resentment?" she said in a later interview, per her biography. "And from my own race and people? There was such a total 'No, you can *not* do it' that frightened the hell out of me."

Lady Sings the Blues, directed by Sidney J. Furie, is certainly a sanitized take on the life of Billie Holiday. Yes, it portrays her addiction to heroin, but it also operates as a love story between Billie and her husband Louis McKay—even though on-screen he's an amalgamation of a few different men in her life. The movie acknowledges her tragic demise while also giving her a happy ending.

Ross purposefully didn't try to do a Billie Holiday impression. She was more interested in absorbing the famed jazz singer, trying to channel the sorrow in her voice for the recordings. (A *New York Times* music critic was unimpressed with the soundtrack on its own, but that didn't stop it from becoming a hit.)

Ross's performance stunned critics. Famously, Roger Ebert went in with all of the raised eyebrows typical of those who believed Ross was underqualified for the part, but he declared it "one of the great performances of 1972." A *Rolling Stone* profile argued that Ross, whose image was carefully constructed by Gordy, "is living proof that stars who really shine are not born, they're professionally made," while also praising her "devastating" performance as "the first time that Diana Ross has been unleashed."

In proving her doubters wrong, Ross had emerged as not just an Oscar nominee but a very likely Oscar winner. She thought she had it locked up, thanks to the positive reinforcement supplied by Gordy. The mogul took Oscar campaigning seriously, figuring if he could bombard voters with images of Ross, she would be victorious. His run of "for your consideration" ads remains a notorious case of Oscar politics gone wrong. His strategy ended up annoying the crowd he most wanted to impress. But he never lost confidence. Gordy even gave Ross a dog the night before the ceremony. It was her birthday. She asked him to name it. He chose "Oscar."

As for her (multiple) outfits, Ross sought out the fashion prowess of Mackie and Ray Aghayan in what was, in some ways, a throwback to the old days of Oscar fashion, when actresses would turn to their costumers for counsel. Mackie and Aghayan, along with Norma Koch, had designed the clothes for *Lady Sings the Blues* and were up for an award themselves on Oscar night. Mackie, best known for his collaborations with Cher, had been dressing Ross since 1969, when he was hired onto an Emmy-winning Supremes TV special. The two ensembles he planned for her span the gamut from of-the-era wacky (the suit) to classic (the dress). The silver jacket and pants could not have been farther from Jane Fonda's menswear the year before. This was not breaking gender norms for solemnity's sake. It was an act of flash, which rubbed some the wrong way. The gown was intended to counter that. Mackie describes it as such: "It had a wonderful little white collar on it. It was very demure, and had little rosebuds embroidered here and there on the dress. She looked beautiful. I mean, Diana looked great in everything." But that image was essentially lost to time, though it was preserved in a sketch from Mackie's archives he provided to me for review. "I think she honestly thought she'd have something elegant to wear as she picked up her Oscar," Mackie recalls. "I mean, you're asking for disappointment. You just are. It's terrible to do that to yourself."

It's hard to deny Liza Minnelli's Oscar win. *Cabaret* is ultimately a more daring, subversive film than *Lady Sings the Blues*, and Minnelli's Sally Bowles is one of the great screen performances of all time. Still, that night in 1973 is remembered by a what-if. What if Ross—or her co-nominee Cicely Tyson—had become the first Black woman to win Best Actress? Was racism at the root of why Ross was ultimately labeled "desperate" for the prize or was it sexism? (Probably both.) Would Ross's iconic outfit be not that suit, but a black dress studded with rosebuds?

CICELY TYSON

(1973)

THE 1973 OSCARS ARE LARGELY REMEMBERED FOR moments like *The Godfather*'s victory, Bob Fosse's directing win, and Marlon Brando's absence. But it was also a monumental occasion. It was the first time two Black women were nominated for Best Actress at the same time. That wouldn't happen again until 2021. (In a curious coincidence, Andra Day was nominated for playing Billie Holiday that year, the same role Ross played in 1973.) Ross competed for the prize alongside Cicely Tyson, who played Rebecca Morgan, mother of the young protagonist in the film *Sounder*.

Tyson, a fashion icon until her death in early 2021, saw the dresses she wore around the promotion of *Sounder* as an extension of her character. She called on her stylist Bill

Whitten, who was most famous for creating Michael Jackson's bedazzled glove, to make ensembles that she imagined Rebecca would have worn if she were a wealthy woman, rather than the wife of a sharecropper in 1933 Louisiana. At the Oscars, Tyson opted for a hairstyle that evoked the period, wearing the waves known as a croquignole. She told the *Hollywood Reporter* that her hairdresser's mother came out of retirement to complete that specific look.

The gown Whitten designed was white and long-sleeved with gray accents. Tyson described it better than I ever could in her memoir. It was "complete with a heart cut-out, lace-trimmed detail across the décolletage. Gracing each sleeve was a glistening row of tiny buttons, with the same buttons stretching down the back. It was absolutely stunning." She accented the wool frock with a fox fur piece, which hung around her neck, the face of the animal on her bodice.

Tyson's view of her style as an extension of Rebecca's was itself a result of her passion for the material. She told the *Christian Science Monitor* at the time that Rebecca was a counter to the many portrayals of Black women in cinema. "The Black woman has always been shown as the stereotype who goes nagging after her husband or putting him down. Or she's a whore, or an addict, or a sex symbol, or she's some empty brain, you know, a vacuous being," she said. "But she's never shown as a human being who has dignity and pride right?" At the ceremony she aimed to give Rebecca the "dignity and pride" that her circumstances would not allow her.

In *Just As I Am*, Tyson describes how unsurprised she was that Minnelli ended up the winner that year. Minnelli was pedigreed in Hollywood: Her father was a celebrated director, her mother was Judy Garland, and at the time she was dating Desi Arnaz Jr., the son of Lucille Ball and Desi Arnaz. You can see Tyson's nonplussed reaction when Minnelli's name is called during the telecast. She even mouths Minnelli's name.

But Tyson was equally frustrated at the way she and Ross were pitted against one another as the two Black actresses in contention. Tyson herself felt no animosity toward Ross, but there was a brewing narrative that they were somehow competing, and clothes played a part in the story. Per Tyson, someone from Ross's team tried to impede the completion of her Oscar dress by hiring Whitten to work on suits for the Jackson 5. She never knew whether Ross was aware of that betrayal, but she wasn't interested in fueling any of the nasty rumors. "I wanted no part in such unpleasantness," she said. "Just Breathing While Black is trouble enough."

As Rebecca Morgan, Tyson exudes kindness and steadfastness in the face of poverty, hunger, and hardship. Her husband is arrested for stealing food to save his family, while she is at the mercy of a racist prison system. Tyson's Oscar nomination, even without a win, came with a sense of immense personal accomplishment, but she extended that honor to the woman she played, who, to her, represented so many women who would never have the opportunity to sit in the Dorothy Chandler Pavilion. In that gown, fur adorning her shoulders, waves in her hair, she was Tyson, yes, but she was also Rebecca—and all the Rebeccas before her.

kids
at the oscars

THE ACADEMY AWARDS ARE NOT REALLY AN EVENT FOR children—the films honored usually feature adult material; the festivities extend past bedtimes. Yet every so often a child becomes the focus of the Oscars' attention. Once in a blue moon a kid gives a performance that's deemed so extraordinary it's hard for the members of the Academy to ignore. The governing body used to have a more formal way of acknowledging the contributions of the young: A juvenile award was handed out sporadically from 1935 through 1961, starting with honors for Shirley Temple, still arguably the most famous child star who ever lived. But that prize has since been relegated to history. Now it's just the select few who manage to compete with the grown-ups, and, occasionally, one of them ends up winning.

What does a child wear when going to the Oscars? Whether she assumes a preternatural adulthood or dresses like she's going to her bat mitzvah, what's certain is that the young's fashion choices have been subject to the same celebration and even scrutiny as their more mature peers.

TATUM O'NEAL

(1974)

In an exhaustive recap of the 1974 Academy Awards ceremony, *Variety* writer Addison Verrill called winner Tatum O'Neal a "moppet"—pretty diminutive for a person who had just won one of the highest honors in her profession: Best Supporting Actress. Verrill wrote of her win for *Paper Moon*: "It was something of a surprise and the moppet's acceptance was disarming." Tatum was 10 years old, the youngest Oscar winner of all time, which she remains to this day. When she went up to collect her trophy—which from certain angles appeared to be nearly half her size—she wore a tuxedo. It was seemingly indebted to Diana Ross's the year prior. But there was something even more—as Verrill had written—"disarming" about seeing a little girl dressed that way. It defied both her age and the norms for her gender. Sure, it was stylish, but it wasn't cute exactly. That was bound to throw a lot of people off.

Why a tux for Tatum? The young O'Neal wanted to emulate Bianca Jagger. The glamorous party girl, a regular at

Studio 54, was having an affair with O'Neal's movie star father Ryan at the time.

O'Neal's mother was an addict who put her daughter and son, Tatum's brother Griffin, in abusive situations. Care of her was eventually transferred to Ryan, who was not much better equipped to take care of the "strange little girl," as Tatum described herself in her memoir *A Paper Life*. One solution was to put her in a movie. He told *People* magazine: "This was the first opportunity to try to channel her energy and mind into something constructive. And give her what she never had enough of—love."

Adapted from the novel *Addie Pray*, Peter Bogdanovich's 1973 film starred the O'Neals as a con artist team during the Great Depression. She's the spunky orphan who picks up the tools of the trade. Despite Ryan's intentions to give her "love" with the movie, it instead fueled his jealousy. He punched her when he discovered she had been nominated and he had not.

In the lead-up to the ceremony, O'Neal followed her father to London where he was filming Stanley Kubrick's *Barry Lyndon*. That's where she became enchanted with Jagger. "I was a big fan of fashion. I was obsessed with clothes," Tatum later told the *Hollywood Reporter*. "Bianca Jagger was my dad's girlfriend at the time, and she wore these suits with little flowers, boots, a cane and these beautiful Tiffany flat diamonds and no bra. I thought, 'That's what I want!' If I could have used a cane, too, I would have. I did have little platform shoes on. My dad got them. He did stuff like that for me."

Her grandmother took her to the designer Nolan Miller to get her little tux custom-made. Standing there with her trophy, she looked even smaller than she was. The award seemed heavy in her hands, and the oversized bow tie dwarfed her head. The outfit was ahead of its time, but it made her seem like she was playing dress-up. In retrospect, it's sad: a little girl emulating the adults who didn't love her. The Oscar was not a triumphant moment for her. She wrote: "There was no fanfare from anyone who mattered to me, so the pride and self-worth I might have gained from what most people would consider a life-defining honor was leached away."

ANNA PAQUIN

(1994)

The easiest thing to remember about Anna Paquin's Oscar win is that she couldn't speak. The 11-year-old actress from New Zealand leapt out of her chair when Gene Hackman revealed that she had beaten the likes of Emma Thompson and Winona Ryder for her work in Jane Campion's *The Piano*. She walked up briskly and could barely see over the podium. The microphone lingered above her head. She breathed heavily, giggling.

Her silence was fitting. After all, *The Piano* was a movie *about* silence. Paquin portrayed a mute woman's daughter, who translates for and betrays her mother (Holly Hunter) when they are forced to move to New Zealand in the epic romance.

It's also symbolic in another respect. It's difficult to find any interviews with Paquin from the time that could explain why she wore a sparkly beret and lace-up boots with a vest over her skirt. She looked like a sprite up there trying to compose herself in order to quickly eke out her thank-you.

Paquin's parents were careful about letting her do press. A 1994 story from the *Los Angeles Times* is described as her "first and only" interview. She discusses mastering the Scottish dialect and bonding with Hunter, who also won an Oscar for her role. Paquin's father explained that he never expected the film to gain the amount of traction it did. "Suddenly, we're dealing with 'Jurassic Piano,'" he said, in a nod to the major blockbuster of the year. "Fortunately for us who are trying to keep Anna a kid a while longer, New Zealand is pretty removed from it all."

Paquin was remarkably innocent for her position. According to the *Pasadena Star-News*, after winning her Oscar she "charmed the cynical pressroom with her lack of sophistication." When asked about her future career she seemed confused about the question. But no amount of protection could stop people from commenting on her outfit. An attempted humor column in the *Tampa Bay-Times* called her beret "tacky."

Looking back, Paquin views the triumph as a distant memory. Asked what she considers her greatest achievement in a 2019 interview with the *Guardian*, she explains that she hopes it hasn't come yet, despite the success she had at such a young age. "My Oscar? That was a combination of Holly Hunter being an amazing actress, Jane being an extraordinary director, and me being in the right place at the right time," she said. "I had no idea what I was doing. It's given me this amazing life, but it's not the highlight of my career." She hadn't yet found her voice.

QUVENZHANÉ WALLIS
(2013)

If O'Neal was trying to simulate adulthood with her Nolan Miller suit, Quvenzhané Wallis emphasized just how much of a child she was with her choice of accessory. Yes, I'm talking about the puppy purse.

Wallis was only five years old when she filmed *Beasts of the Southern Wild* and nine when she was nominated for an Oscar for her performance as an almost feral child in the magically realist saga about the Louisiana Bayou that had echoes of Hurricane Katrina. And she seemed like very much a kid. Wallis showed up to every event that Oscar season with a stuffed puppy purse.

The puppy purses quickly became a media phenomenon. Wallis would appear in a dainty little dress wearing flat Mary Janes with a little dog on her arm. Some had floppy ears. One was a bulldog. One had pink fur. Even at her age, she was well aware of the statement she was making. She told Ellen DeGeneres in an interview that the puppy bags, which were produced by a brand appropriately named Poochie & Co., were her "signature," and of course she would be carrying one on the big night. After all, she owned about 20 of them.

On the red carpet, she wore a midnight blue floor-length gown, a little more formal than her usual style. Her puppy also dressed up for the occasion. The little plush terrier-looking animal wore a tiara and had a pint-sized dress of its own. The aesthetic was, for lack of a better description, ridiculously adorable.

Wallis's penchant for puppies was a constant reminder to her nominated peers and the audience watching that she really was a child, which is why the injustice she endured during the ceremony stung all the more.

The satirical *Onion* newspaper was live tweeting the ceremony when whoever was manning the accounted decided to joke: "Everyone else seems afraid to say it, but that Quvenzhané Wallis is kind of a cunt, right?" The condemnation of the undeniably offensive tweet was quick. In a supremely misguided attempt at jest, the publication ended up calling a young girl of color one of the worst insults that could possibly be hurled. In its ignorance it was also racially pointed: As one person noted, a white child star like Dakota Fanning was never assaulted with that kind of language. The *Onion* apologized, a rarity for the institution, but the damage was done: Wallis's experience at the Academy Awards would not be associated with the charming puppy purses. Rather, its legacy would be cemented by a heinous slur.

edy williams

(1986)

THERE'S NO GOOD REASON WHY EDY WILLIAMS should have attended the Oscars all the years she attended the Oscars. And Edy Williams, despite never having been nominated for an Oscar, attended the Oscars a lot between the early 1970s and the late 1990s. Williams and her ensembles were a near constant fixture of the event during this two-decade span. The first time she went she wore a leopard-print bikini. In 1986, she wore pearls and not much else.

The look was wild. Williams appeared wearing a breast-plate of pearls that hung on her body, barely covering her nipples, just grazing her areolas. She carried a purple shawl slung over her shoulder and wore lace gloves. It was a garment—if you even want to call it that—that would seem at home in Las Vegas or *maybe* at the MTV Video Music Awards.

Other examples of her sartorial sneak attacks on the Academy's front lawn can be best described as "slutty Little Bo Peep," "just pasties," and "one boob out." A couple times she brought dogs along with her. But whatever you want to say about Edy Williams's style—that it was trashy or inappropriate or scandalous—it was certainly always entertaining, a reminder that on an evening when Hollywood is arguably the most up its own ass, some people are just there to have a good time and raise a few eyebrows.

Of all the people this book covers, Williams is arguably the most obscure. Her type of stardom, while analogous to some of her successors in the reality TV realm, has largely passed. Her credits are cult favorites. But for a while she was just as much a part of the fabric of the Academy Awards red carpet scene as Joan Rivers.

So who is Edy Williams? Technically, she is an actress. Her first listed credit was as a "chorus girl" in a 1962 episode of *The Twilight Zone*, and she bounced around in bit parts on television shows like *Batman*, *The Man from U.N.C.L.E.*, and *The Beverly Hillbillies*. Williams's best-known credit came in 1970 when she played porn star Ashley St. Ives in Russ Meyer's *Beyond the Valley of the Dolls*. With a flowing mound of hair, she seduces the male protagonist, who has come to Los Angeles to manage his girlfriend's rock band. Ashley has sex with him in a Rolls-Royce all the while cooing, "Nothing like a Rolls."

Taking its name from Jacqueline Susann's seminal novel about a group of women and their misadventures in Hollywood, *Beyond the Valley of the Dolls*, cowritten by the critic Roger Ebert, is an exercise in satire and camp. It's over-the-top in a self-aware way, packed with female nudity and hilariously theatrical dialogue. It's smutty, yes, but it's also not serious about its smuttiness. In that sense it's a good analogue for Edy Williams's entire ethos. She was *Beyond the Valley of the Dolls* in human form: Constantly pushing boundaries while also making you question just how in on the joke she was.

Williams married her director Meyer the same year *Beyond the Valley of the Dolls* was released, and they divorced a mere five years later. In 1974, Williams began her dual annual traditions of appearing at both the Cannes Film Festival and the Oscars and making a scene.

In 1981, Ebert himself tried to sum up the place Williams occupied in the Hollywood ecosystem in a story in the *Washington Post*. She was a "starlet" in the old-fashioned sense, someone who was under contract with a movie studio, but not the biggest star. Williams herself was with 20th Century Fox until 1971, one of the last of her breed. Ebert described the "duties" of the starlet as such: "They had to look gorgeous, attend acting classes, play bit parts in movies and, most important, pose for thousands of cheesecake photographs and be on call 24 hours a day for the opening of a supermarket, the christening of a boat or the dedication of a shopping center." There's something almost tragic about the way Ebert writes about Williams. Her stunts, many of which involved nudity, were all an effort to get discovered, to rise higher than her status. At the same time, Williams wasn't completely unaware of how she was perceived. She thrived on shock value.

Interviews with Williams are actually scarce. The webpage dedicated to her career has disappeared into the internet ether. But in 1986, shortly after the Oscars, she did try to defend herself, albeit on a hostile platform. She went on the talk show hosted by conservative Wally George, who charged her with dressing "disgracefully" at what is "supposed to be a classy very upbeat affair." The chyron branded her "Lady Lust," the title of a movie she appeared in in 1984, and she smiled as the crowd in the audience jeered at her. She explained, "I have a good sense of humor." Yes, Edy Williams knew she was having a laugh at the Academy Awards when she arrived at the Dorothy Chandler Pavilion wearing some strings of pearls.

Opinions on Edy's appearance in 1986 were divided in the letters to the editor section of the *Los Angeles Times*. One Greg Shaw wrote in: "In response to the controversy concerning the eternal starlet, Edy Williams: the only reason I watch the early arrivals at the Oscars each year is to see Edy Williams. She is one of a kind, a true survivor of Hollywood glamour. She is smart and experienced and has a fabulous face and body." Another commenter sneered at her, even while giving her "credit" for essentially being a social climber. "Granted, she doesn't wear very much in the way of a gown, but, hey, every year this woman somehow manages to squeeze through the bars and gates of Camarillo (a feat in itself) to get to the Dorothy Chandler."

In 1986, Williams wasn't even that out of place. Sure, it was a little more highbrow, but Cher wore a Bob Mackie gown that also evoked a showgirl aesthetic, with a towering headdress and a bare midriff. But Edy Williams was not Cher and never would be. She was a hanger-on, not really a has-been, but a never-been grasping for her chance in the bright lights. She was an attention seeker ahead of her time. Williams would have thrived in a Hollywood where the Kardashians or the Real Housewives had clout. She would have been cheered when she fired back at Wally George: "What's wrong with a woman showing off her body?" (Though, admittedly, right-wing blowhards would probably still have a problem with her even today.) She would have been hailed as a subversive genius. Sure, it wasn't "classy," but who cares when it's this much fun?

cher

(1988)

B Y THE TIME CHER WAS NOMINATED FOR AN ACADEMY
Award for Best Actress for her work in 1987's *Moon
struck* she had already shocked the Oscar crowd with
a wonderfully insane outfit. At the 1986 Oscars Cher did the
most Cher thing you could possibly imagine. She showed up in
a towering feathered headdress, midriff bare, both the top and
bottom accentuated by triangular hems, like teeth chomping

on her stomach. The showgirl-
inspired outfit was created by
her longtime collaborator, the
designer Bob Mackie, who
would later tell the *New Yorker*
that it was conceived at least
a little bit out of vengeance.
That season, Cher had starred
in Peter Bogdanovich's film
Mask, playing the mother of a
disfigured teenager. She had

won Best Actress at Cannes but was snubbed at the Oscars. "She was pissed off, because she didn't get nominated for 'Mask,'" Mackie said. "There were a lot of people who said, 'That's not fashion!' And I said, 'Of course it's not fashion. It's a crazy getup for attention.' And it did get attention—people talk about it still." Mackie would recall to me in a phone call that they met about the design at her then-boyfriend Tom Cruise's New York apartment. "She said, 'I don't want to look like a housewife in an evening gown,'" he remembers. "We never have to worry about that."

By the time Cher did get nominated two years later, she had a big act to follow in the fashion department: her own. Cher is one of those performers who seems to be constantly in the midst of a renaissance, and the mid-to-late 1980s was no different. She had left Sonny Bono and her variety show days long behind, become a successful solo act as a pop star, and was now well into her serious actress phase, beginning with her supporting role in Mike Nichols's 1983 based-on-real-life drama *Silkwood*, which had netted her a Best Supporting Actress nomination. She lost. Cher both wanted an Oscar and also wanted to sort of say "fuck the Oscars" at the same time.

In *Moonstruck* Cher plays Loretta Castorini, a widow from a big Italian family with a thick New York accent. In the first bit of the film her hair is peppered with gray. She doesn't wear makeup. She's marrying a loser of a man—sweet, but nervous and unexciting—who asks her to contact his long-lost brother while he's in Italy tending to his dying mother. Loretta does as he requests and finds Ronny Cammareri (Nicolas Cage) in the ovens of a local bakery. It turns out that he hates his brother, Loretta's fiancé, whom he claims is responsible for the loss of his hand and his former bride-to-be. Ronny and Loretta fall in love. It's not often that romantic comedies get the respect they deserve at the Oscars, but Cher's performance in *Moonstruck* is undeniable. She's both iconic and makes it possible to forget that she's an icon herself.

Cher had a storied history with the Oscars going back to the 1960s, when she was on the arm of Bono, but she always insisted that she do them her way, even with the knowledge that it might ultimately cost her in the long run. Her decision to wear the intentionally ludicrous getup in 1986 was a reaction to those who thought she was too extravagant, too much of a pop star to be taken seriously as an actress. "I wasn't going to go at all," she told the *New York Times* back in 1987. "And then they asked me to present, these people who had just said, 'No, you can't be one of us.' I thought, 'O.K., you can go in a simple black dress and be just like everyone else.' But then I decided, 'I'm going to remind them of what they don't like about me.'"

She was aware there might be consequences. In a conversation with *Film Comment* before her nomination for *Moonstruck*, she talked about what she called the "trashy part" of her personality. "I continue to do really stupid things—like dress the way I dressed at the Academy Awards . . ." The interviewer interrupted her to ask whether she really thought that was stupid. "No, I thought it was great," she continued. "But as far as winning friends and influencing people, it's stupid. But that's just always going to be me, it's going to be the way I do stuff because I just have a hard time with authority." She admitted that she was prepared to "live" with the fact that her antics could mean she might not hold a trophy one day.

But that wasn't the case. She had tough competition: Her *Silkwood* costar and friend Meryl Streep in *Ironweed*, Holly Hunter in *Broadcast News*, and Glenn Close in *Fatal Attraction*, but she was a Golden Globe winner going into the April ceremony. The biggest question was not whether she would win, but, yes, what she would wear. The *Los Angeles Times* breathlessly reported: "There's only one fashion question worth asking about this year's Academy Awards show: What's Cher going to wear Monday night?" Would she once again opt for shock and awe? Or something more conservative to appease the crowd that had presumably cast ballots for her? Mackie dished on what Cher had in mind: "It's all see-through and black, and what you'd expect of Cher." He would later tell me that it was "like a beautiful period dress—except there was no underwear." If you made the gown opaque, it would look like something anyone would wear, really. But with her belly button on display, and the fabric merely a delivery service for thousands of beads, it was just cheeky enough, while still maintaining the kind of elegance you would expect from a winner. The Associated Press called it "far from modest." She lost an earring made of gunmetal on the way to the stage, a mistake that made her look even cooler in retrospect.

Nothing was going to stop Cher from being Cher. A year later, having achieved the highest honor in the film industry, she went back to dominate the pop world with her single "If I Could Turn Back Time." She kept the sheer theme going. The video features Cher clad in a leather jacket and a barely there bodysuit on a battleship surrounded by a bunch of sailors.

sharon stone

(1996)

T HE PRESS DIDN'T REALLY KNOW WHAT TO MAKE of Sharon Stone around the time of her awards run for 1995's *Casino*. She was the sexpot who had steamed up the screen as a slippery murder suspect in *Basic Instinct*. Following that breakout, her career had taken a downward spiral with a series of flops, but she had returned in great form with Martin Scorsese's Vegas gangster epic as Ginger, the drug-addicted moll whom Robert De Niro's gangster marries and then divorces. She's described in profiles from the time as both alluring and erratic, a puzzle to be solved. "I think for a long time people just did not know what to do with me," she told the *Los Angeles Times*. "I looked like a Barbie doll and then I had this voice like I spend my life in a bar and then I said these things that were alarming and had ideas that didn't make sense."

Perhaps nothing better represented the contradictions of Sharon Stone than what she wore to the 1996 Oscars, where

she was up for Best Actress thanks to her role in the Scorsese picture. She hit the carpet in a floor-length Armani tuxedo dress, used as a jacket over a Valentino skirt, and, most shockingly, a Gap turtleneck. Stone had a perfectly good reason for putting together these items—a fashion disaster involving her planned attire that she'd later describe in interviews—but even without context, the outfit embodied Stone's appeal: both accessible and untouchable, populist and dramatic.

Years later, Stone would explain exactly what led her to pull the Gap shirt out of her closet. In a 2020 interview for Naomi Campbell's YouTube talk show, she detailed the whole story. She was supposed to wear Vera Wang, who was designing custom gowns for her. The first option wasn't quite working, the malleable fabric kept changing. The second was pink, and it was all ready to go, but suffered a cruel fate. "We were making this other great dress, this pink dress, and it came, and the FedEx guy dropped it out of the back of his truck and backed over it," she said. "The box broke open and the dress had a black tire track down the whole of the front of the dress. The day before the Oscars." She got ahold of costume designer Ellen Mirojnick, the woman responsible for what was up to that point her most famous outfit: that slinky white number from the interrogation scene in *Basic Instinct*. Mirojnick devised a plan. She asked Stone to get her favorite clothes from the closet. Stone, frazzled, decided to start pulling everything black in what she would call a "Johnny Cash impulse," and Mirojnick, working her magic, came up with the concept. To top it off, Stone grabbed a gardenia from her garden.

The next day, the Associated Press ran a short article, featured in newspapers across the country, about Stone's top. It noted that it cost only $22 and was part of a 1995 line that had since gone out of stock. The Gap spokeswoman was thrilled. "She just wanted to be comfortable," she said of Stone. Stone would later affirm that in her recollection of the evening. "This thing, this turn of events, seemed not only to free me but to free my inner artist, to know I was there not because of a dress or because of the show, but because of my work," she wrote in her 2021 memoir *The Beauty of Living Twice*. "I felt more grounded in that Gap turtleneck than I had in a lot of other hard-to-carry dresses. It taught me that comfort is the most important step to style."

Stone chose Gap at the height of its trendiness. In the early 1990s, the retailer was winning over consumers with its basics and savvy marketing campaigns. Starting in 1988, with its "Individuals of Style" campaign, the brand positioned itself as casual wear for trendy intellectuals. The ads featured the likes of Spike Lee and Joan Didion wearing the merchandise, photographed by Annie Leibovitz. Stone's choice was used as an example of powerful women rejecting formalwear for clothes that were more livable and cheaper. A report in the *New York Times* found that women were spending less money on fashion in general in the early '90s. "If there is any doubt that casual, inexpensive dressing has become a status symbol, reflect on the uber sex goddess Sharon Stone, who appeared onstage at the Oscars this year wearing not her signature Valentino but a black Gap turtleneck," the article read. Of course, that's more than a little disingenuous. After all, Stone was still wearing Valentino—just a piece from the ready-to-wear collection from her own closet. Perhaps the most notable word choice worth examining in that excerpt is not the rejection of Valentino, but the shock in the paper of record that this "uber sex goddess" was wearing plain old Gap.

All the press orbiting Stone at the time was reckoning with that "uber sex goddess" image, just as she herself was. She appeared in the March 1996 issue of *Vanity Fair*, on newsstands the same month as the Oscars. Writer Lloyd Grove wrote: "Never mind her tough-gal reputation (Sharon 'Stones,' a studio wag once dubbed her), she is suddenly that most fragile of Hollywood creatures—a movie star in transition. As she looks forward this month to her 38th birthday, and calculates her strategy for stardom in middle age, Stone is striving to reinvent herself—to move from moaning siren to serious artiste. The transformation is not always seamless." Stone was a tabloid fixation at the time with a quote-unquote difficult reputation. But even though everyone had seen the work she did in *Casino*—a towering performance that is, yes, sexy, but also fearsome and deeply sad—being hot was something that Stone had to rise above.

As Bob Dole ran for president, touting family values and igniting a right-wing panic regarding sex and violence in Hollywood, Stone was forced to defend her choice of roles, even in front of the National Press Club. (During the trip, the press derided her quote-unquote diva behavior.) The female Oscar nominees that year ignited a debate on the other side of the political aisle as well. The *New York Times* spoke to feminist critics taking stock of the fact that three of the women nominated, including Stone, were playing prostitutes. "It's hooker chic," the film critic Molly Haskell told the *Times*. "In some ways it's male and female fantasies coinciding. It's male projections of the kind of women they think they'd like. And for actresses it's a juicy role, a stretch, a chance to be bad and desirable and rebellious." In Hollywood you're pegged as either a virgin, a whore, or old, and Stone had played a whore and was getting older.

The following years weren't kind to Stone. She wasn't flooded with roles of Ginger's caliber. She had health problems. She remained just as fierce and gorgeous as ever but was even more inscrutable. She was too thoroughly herself to fit into her prescribed box, too much of a wild card, too much of a Gap turtleneck at the Oscars.

gwyneth paltrow

and

matt stone

(1999/2000)

THIS IS THE TALE OF TWO PEOPLE WEARING THE same dress. One was Gwyneth Paltrow, when she won Best Actress for her performance in the 1998 film *Shakespeare in Love.* The other was *South Park* creator Matt Stone, who showed up in a replica of that dress a year later when "Blame Canada" from *South Park: Bigger, Longer & Uncut* was nominated for Best Original Song.

Gwyneth's gown was the first I ever remember loving. I distinctly recall the morning after the ceremony, sitting in my elementary school's computer room, sketching the garment for my best friend. Of course, it would appeal to an eight-year-old: The Ralph Lauren design had tiny spaghetti straps, upon which hung a loose V-neck bodice. Below that was a wide skirt, all in a bubblegum pink hue. Oh yes, the pink was a big part of the appeal for me. The dress was a child's fantasy of what a movie star should look like: billowing and princess-y.

"I just wanted to look sweet," Paltrow said of her choice, and while it captivated me as a kid, to some the look was almost too sugary, yet another reason to roll eyes at Paltrow.

These were the early days of Gwyneth skepticism. It was long before she would become known for popularizing the phrase "conscious uncoupling" and peddling overly expensive wares on Goop, but she was still polarizing. Paltrow was at the center of mega producer, and now convicted sex criminal, Harvey Weinstein's notorious campaign for *Shakespeare in Love*. The movie, a frothy confection that I nonetheless love, was seen as the undeserving alternate pitted against Steven Spielberg's more worthy *Saving Private Ryan*, and bolstered by the aggressive, nasty tactics of Weinstein and his brother Bob. Gwyneth, a daughter of Hollywood, was an easy target for the derision. At the Independent Spirit Awards, which traditionally take place the night before the Oscars, actress Illeana Douglas quipped that Harvey and Bob Weinstein didn't attend an event because they were "pressing Gwynnie's dress."

For her part, Gwyneth wanted to look feminine, maybe even innocent, given the chatter. According to the book *Made for Each Other: Fashion and the Academy Awards*, designers were clamoring to have Gwyneth wear their attire. In a video for *Vogue* revisiting her most famous outfits, Paltrow explained she was perusing Ralph Lauren's look book when she came across a pink taffeta skirt, which she described as "very me." She called and asked to borrow it, and the designer offered to make her something custom. During the lead-up to the big night, Gwyneth was at the Shutters on the Beach hotel in Santa Monica with her mom, Blythe Danner, and some friends. She had already collected a Golden Globe and a SAG Award. If you go by the account in *Made for Each Other*, she was debating between the Ralph and a Celine two-piece until the last moments. "When you are with your girlfriends, and you try on this pretty pink dress, and you think it is so great, so pretty," she reportedly said. She ditched the bustier that was originally affixed to the gown in favor of comfort and a looser style that gave the ensemble just a hint of 1990s grunge.

Reactions were immediately divided. In *Entertainment Weekly*'s style recap, the fashion critics surveyed cooed over it ("Fantastic!" "Perfect!"), while the omniscient voice of the publication threw daggers: "We think Gwyneth's cue-ball hairdo was too severe; her dress hung too low. (Get thee to a tailor, quick!)" The controversial cultural critic Camille Paglia was ruthless in *Salon*. Noting that Joan Rivers had compared

Gwyneth to Grace Kelly, Paglia snapped, "For the entire evening, big-jawed Paltrow, with her nasal, teeth-clenching Lisa Kudrow style, looks like a Green Bay Packers cheesehead tottering atop a mushy pink Hostess cupcake." Loved or hated, for something so simple, the dress quickly gained a reputation. A gossip item in the *New York Daily News* quoted Monica Lewinsky at the *Vanity Fair* Oscar party, quipping, "Finally, a dress more famous than mine." Even Paltrow's own mom later told *Us* that it "didn't fit her very well." And this is all to say nothing of the criticisms of Paltrow's speech—familiar jabs about the cracks in her voice being insincere.

What truly was going through Paltrow's head is hard to say. In 2017, she came forward to tell the *New York Times* that she too had been sexually harassed by Weinstein, the man she thanks effusively in that speech. Perhaps the "sweet" dress was a defense mechanism to combat the sourness orbiting her.

The very next year she became the butt of another joke. Matt Stone's *South Park* collaborator Trey Parker was the official nominee, along with composer Marc Shaiman, but Stone came along for the ride. Parker and Stone's "fuck everything" libertarian attitude certainly didn't align with the pomp and circumstance of the Oscars. They decided to go to the ceremony in their own way, with some help from a couple of hits of what they later revealed to be acid. "We were so, like, punk rock—you know, like, against all of that stuff," Stone told the *Hollywood Reporter* in 2016. "But Trey was nominated for [a best original song Oscar], and that's cool. So how do you go but not go? How do you not be a part of it? Drugs." So they got high and stepped onto the red carpet in famous dresses.

Parker dressed in the extremely low-cut Versace dress Jennifer Lopez had worn at the Grammys just months before. In 2000—and probably to this day—it was the most famous garment ever worn. It was the fabric responsible for the start of Google Images. Stone chose Gwyneth's Ralph. A year before that pink was a symbol of the Hollywood machine at its most powerful and the Oscars at their most serious. On Stone it became a sign of just how silly it all was. It's unlikely that any woman would even dare to make a mockery of two of the most powerful people in their industry, Lopez and Paltrow, in such a public way, but Stone and Parker wielded their male privilege and fuck-all attitude to cause havoc.

Joan Rivers was clearly entertained by the guys on the red carpet. "Will you change for the parties or are you smart enough to get that this is a great photo op?" she asked. Stone later explained that while some of the celebs that passed them by were tickled by their attire—Michael Caine, for instance— others were not so amused. Gloria Estefan was "super-pissed," he said. And why shouldn't she be? They were being held to different standards than everyone else there. But what's most telling is the effort that went into preparing the gag, despite the fact that they were also tripping balls. "It takes a lot of energy to be that rebellious," Stone said. "It took so much energy to get those dresses made and all that stuff."

That is to say: Taunt Gwyneth all you want. Mock her demure style, and her potential crocodile tears. But it's just as hard to emulate her as it is easy to make fun of her.

angelina jolie, two ways

(2000/2012)

IF YOU ASKED SOMEONE TO NAME AN ICONIC ANGELINA Jolie Oscar dress, you would probably get one of two answers. Though Jolie's been to the Oscars numerous times—starting when she was a child and attending with her nominated father Jon Voight in 1986—there is a pair of ensembles that has permeated the pop cultural landscape in a way none of her other looks have. The first was in 2000, when she was nominated and won for her performance in *Girl, Interrupted*. Jolie showed up in a skintight black gown designed by Marc Bouwer, covering every inch of her body in fabric but still leaving little to the imagination. Her hair was dyed nearly black and elongated with extensions. Most people compared her to Morticia Addams. Elvira could also work as a description.

Years later there's Jolie's other most famous Oscar look. In 2000, Jolie looked malleable, her body gliding across the carpet and, notoriously, into the arms of her brother. She looked like she could wilt if she wanted to, dissolve into liquid. Not so in 2012. Jolie arrived in Atelier Versace, almost as if she had been cast into stone. She was the epitome of statuesque. Her head was erect, her arms toned, and, of course, her right leg jutted out stiffly from a thigh-high slit. That leg became an immediate meme, affixed onto all sorts of images, including the Statue of Liberty.

If Jolie in 2000 was all spontaneity, declaring to many people's shock how "in love" she was with her brother, Jolie in 2012 was practiced. No longer was she the goth girl talking about wearing vials of Billy Bob Thornton's blood around her neck. She was a director, activist, and mother to children, both biological and adopted, with Brad Pitt, the *other* biggest movie star alive. They were the king and queen of this place. And she looked regal, almost waxy, like she should be in a museum.

Arguably no star has changed more radically during her time in the public eye than Angelina Jolie. When she first became famous in the late 1990s, she was known for her unpredictability. She married Jonny Lee Miller in 1996 in rubber pants and a T-shirt with his name written on it in blood. A 1999 *Rolling Stone* profile opens with her showing off her tattoos and discussing her bisexuality. She was, yes, the daughter of a very famous actor, but she was also dangerous in a way few ingenues were.

Her role in *Girl, Interrupted* capitalized on this. With blonde hair, she is seductive as the sociopathic rebel Winona Ryder's protagonist meets in a psychiatric hospital in 1967. Despite a cast filled with some of the most fascinating actresses of her generation, as Lisa, Jolie is the most captivating person on-screen, mean and teasing, yet someone to whom you can't help but be drawn.

Lisa was also the type of person the public assumed Angelina Jolie was at the time: uninhibited, maybe a little unstable. And Angelina Jolie did nothing to dissuade people of that notion. On the red carpet, when Tyra Banks asked her how she "transformed herself" for the part, she said, "all those deep dark secrets. I went into a scary place and stayed there for a while." Which brings us to her Morticia Addams look. She looked like a harbinger of evil, not glory. One paper deemed the outfit "weird but memorable"; another called her a "fashion victim."

Her outfit was strange, but not scandalous. What *was* scandalous was the fact that she seemed intent on professing her love for her brother, which culminated in a kiss at the *Vanity Fair* party following the ceremony. In photos from the event it looked like they were making out, which wasn't really the case.

"Angelina had a reputation as a rebellious young actress, so I think the kiss was seen in context of her being a bit of a wild child," Hollywood Life founder Bonnie Fuller told *Bustle* for an oral history of that moment. "Apparently, it was a very quick kiss—which you can't tell by looking at the photo." The combination of the look and the kiss branded Jolie as an incestuous sexpot obsessed with blood.

But Jolie quickly started to evolve her image. A year after her Oscar win she became a UN Goodwill ambassador. The following year she adopted her first child, Maddox, from Cambodia, the country where she focused the majority of her humanitarian attentions. Her relationship with Pitt started as a rumored affair when he was still married to Jennifer Aniston, but by the time 2012 rolled around that felt to many like ancient history. Pitt and Jolie were not yet married, but he had become a legal parent to her adopted children, and they had had three of their own together. She was slowing down her appearances in films, transitioning into work as a director. The previous year she wrote and directed her first feature, *In the Land of Blood and Honey*. It didn't make a mark at the Oscars, but it had netted a Golden Globe nomination for Best Foreign Language Film.

In some ways, the 2012 Oscars were her debut not as an actress, but as a filmmaker, striving to tell stories about war-torn lands. She later explained that she chose the Versace gown because it was more comfortable than her other option. It's curious reasoning because Jolie didn't look very comfortable. She was constantly posing. Though "showing leg" can often be sexy, in this case it wasn't. It almost felt obligatory. Even baring skin, she felt guarded. The stance was less one of seduction than one of power, as if she could wield that leg at any moment and step on your neck.

In 12 years' time, Jolie went from a woman whose lack of filter was one of her defining features to someone who seemed like she was all filter. She began as a wild card who would blurt out whatever was on her mind, wearing a getup that looked like every kid's idea of someone scary. She ended up as a matron, fiercely protective of her image, never a hair, or leg, out of place.

björk

(2001)

NOT ONLY IS BJÖRK'S SWAN DRESS PERHAPS THE most famous of any in this book, it's also the only one to have been on display at both the Metropolitan Museum of Art and MoMA. It's pretty clear now that Marjan Pejoski's creation is a bona fide work of art, an avant-garde fashion statement worn by a performer like no other. And yet, the swan dress is still emblematic of the "worst dressed list." It has, yes, been deemed worthy of exhibition by two of the most prestigious institutions in the world, and yet it's also a joke—and maybe it was always intended that way.

In retrospect, perhaps the strangest thing about the swan dress is that Björk wore it to be honored for her work in one of the most depressing movies of all time: Lars von Trier's *Dancer in the Dark*. The Icelandic singer-songwriter was nominated alongside Radiohead's Thom Yorke for Best Original Song for "I've Seen It All," a ballad sung on-screen by her character Selma, a woman with a degenerative eye disorder who is taken advantage of and ultimately framed for and convicted of

murder. At the end of the film she is executed. Not light, swan dress-type stuff. The casual pop culture aficionado might not even be able to name the reason Björk was in attendance that night in 2001. Once she stepped onto the red carpet, her skirt pluming, the swan dress was all that mattered.

Björk was always going to be too cool for the Oscars. She rose to fame in the early 1990s with music that transcended genre. Her work was always adjacent to the film world. With the likes of Michel Gondry and Spike Jonze, she made some of the most creatively ambitious videos of all time, some of which referenced classic movie musicals but still existed just slightly outside of the mainstream.

The 2001 ceremony—which honored the movies of 2000— was representative of an industry caught at a crossroads between blockbusters and independent films. On the one hand there was *Gladiator*, a Ridley Scott crowd-pleaser that anointed Russell Crowe the next big thing. But it competed against not one but two films from Steven Soderbergh, who had emerged from the indie world, as well as *Crouching Tiger, Hidden Dragon*, Ang Lee's ode to wuxia. America's sweetheart Julia Roberts finally got her trophy, while relative unknown Marcia Gay Harden surprised everyone by winning Best Supporting Actress for *Pollock*.

Björk had been awarded a Best Actress prize earlier in the year when *Dancer in the Dark* premiered at Cannes, but she was aware of her interloper status when she stepped onto the red carpet. Asked during the pre-show about what her first time acting was like, she demurely said, "I prefer the music, but it was great to try it once." (The question wasn't exactly accurate: She had made the 1990 film *The Juniper Tree* before *Dancer in the Dark*.) The host remarked that her dress was a "rather unusual creation." She petted her stomach, "My friend made it," she said without elaboration, a coy smile on her face.

Almost immediately the jokes about the swan dress started. The night's emcee, Steve Martin, managed to work it into his duties, saying, "I was going to wear my swan too, but it was so last year." Hosting the Emmys later in 2001, Ellen DeGeneres came out wearing a replica of the dress. "I guess this is business casual," she quipped, before going into an extended bit riffing on the concept of wearing white after Labor Day. Marlon and Shawn Wayans wore swan dresses in the goofy climax of *White Chicks*, released in 2004. Nearly 12 years later, there were still swan dress jokes to be made—about how many swan dress jokes had been made. "I'm like the following joke about Björk's swan dress: Tired," the character Tracy Jordan says in an episode of *30 Rock* from the show's seventh season in 2013.

But to make fun of the swan dress is also to imply that Björk was not in on the joke, which would be severely underestimating Björk. Björk knew exactly what she was doing. If she didn't, would she have brought eggs to "lay" on the carpet as she walked down it? "It was really funny, cos [sic] the life-guards [interpreted to mean security guards] would pick them up and run after me with their walkie-talkies: 'Excuse me, miss, you dropped this!'" she told the *Sunday Times* in 2004. "C'mon, you don't bring eggs unless you want to take the piss, right? I was actually amazed at how many people thought I was seri-ous. I didn't mean to cause a riot!" She would continue to make it clear that she found the whole thing actually very amusing. When the dress was on display at MoMA during a retrospective of her career, she told *Time*: "They were almost going to put a red carpet, but then, somebody talked us out of that. It would have been funny, though." Explaining why the garment was included in the exhibit, then-chief curator at large of MoMA Klaus Biesenbach told the *New York Times* that it "reflects a certain independent spirit, a punk spirit, an unexpected sur-prising spirit—that she can be part of the establishment and will still surprise and challenge everyone."

She kept the dress on for the entire night, even when she performed "I've Seen It All." The whimsy of the outfit clashed with the minor keys of the song. That she didn't change for her number was one of the reasons *Entertainment Weekly* put her on the "worst dressed" list, under the moniker "Ugly Duck-ling." "It was birdbrained of her to keep it on for her performance," the caption read. "The goofy swan detracted from the poignancy of her song." Björk didn't really have anything to lose. Bob Dylan was ultimately the victor with his song from *Wonder Boys*.

For over a decade now, the swan dress has been the pre-eminent example of bad Oscar fashion. Even as it has risen in estimation, entering the hallowed halls of the palaces of art, it still remains entrenched on listicles from E!. It's hard to imagine that the dress would have had the same reception if Björk had debuted it in the 2010s, after the viewing public had witnessed Lady Gaga in meat, rather than at the turn of the century. Björk, of course, paved the way for all of Gaga's sartorial experiments, but even that provocateur went traditional when she attended the Oscars. The swan dress seems like it should conform to the rules of propriety. It's fairly demure. The puffy skirt is almost ladylike. But it's just kooky enough to be radical. Reminiscing about the design, Pejoski told the *Hollywood Reporter*: "With the Oscars, there's a uniform, like the police. Björk was definitely outside the box. Without people like her, it would be boring." Biesenbach described the dress as "political." Perhaps it did end up challenging establishment norms, but it was also something of a joke. And a good one at that.

musicians
at the Oscars

WHEN IT COMES TO FASHION, THE WORLDS OF MUSIC AND movies are in different universes. Musicians adhere to their personal styles above all else, making the red carpets for the likes of the Grammys or the VMAs more erratic than anything the Oscars have to offer. Björk was not the only celeb attending because of her inclusion in the original song category who tested the boundaries of Oscar style. Here are some others.

CELINE DION

(1998)

What do you wear when the movie you're representing contains what is possibly one of the most iconic pieces of jewelry of all time? That piece of jewelry, of course. Celine Dion, known for her outré fashion, went simple when it came time to sing "My Heart Will Go On" from *Titanic* at the 1997 awards. Dion was not actually nominated for an Oscar for "My Heart Will Go On," given that she did not write it. She was just there to perform. She had two black dresses. One with a V-neck for the red carpet, another with a turtleneck for the performance. But the true star was the $2.2 million replica of the Heart of the Ocean sapphire from the film sitting on her neck like a searchlight. Inspired by the film, it was designed by the jeweler Asprey & Garrard and encrusted with diamonds. The next year she could dress as goofily as her heart desired, and she did, wearing a white backward John Galliano tux and a fedora.

LUIS RESTO

(2003)

Eminem didn't show up when his juggernaut of a song "Lose Yourself" from *8 Mile* won Best Original Song in 2003. But his cowriter Luis Resto did, in a Detroit Pistons jersey. The choice was symbolic, not sloppy, as some may have assumed. Eminem is from Detroit; *8 Mile* was an homage to his roots. But Resto's attire was also maybe just a little too cool for school. The rapper himself was the only original song nominee not to perform or attend, and his representative eschewed the typical Oscar-wear for this overly chill look. *E! News* deemed Resto's attire "un-celebrity like," but he didn't create a scandal like, say, *Mad Max: Fury Road* costume designer Jenny Beavan did when she showed up in a motorcycle jacket (see page 182).

SUFJAN STEVENS

(2018)

The art pop singer-songwriter Sufjan Stevens later said he was mortified performing at the Oscars. He told the *Guardian* it was "traumatizing" and "everything I hate about America and popular culture." But onstage in a Gucci jacket with pink stripes and dragons adorning his shoulders, he was magic. Bringing an all-star team of musicians—Chris Thile, St. Vincent, and Moses Sumney—he performed "Mystery of Love," the mystically sad song from *Call Me by Your Name*. His look was celebrated on social media as an ethereal triumph.

halle berry

(2002)

HALLE BERRY NEEDED A HISTORIC DRESS FOR A historic win. Heading into March 24, 2002, Berry was poised to become the first Black woman to win Best Actress. It was a moment that was long overdue. Berry herself had played Dorothy Dandridge, the first Black woman even nominated for the prize for 1954's *Carmen Jones*, a television movie that netted her an Emmy.

The gown was in so many ways the least important part of Berry's moment. It was outranked by the surge of her emotion; by her tearful speech in which she thanked the women that came before her: Dandridge, Lena Horne, Diahann Carroll, as well as her peers Jada Pinkett Smith and Angela Bassett. But, of course, the dress was also a crucial part of the imagery of that night.

Berry was showered with options before the show, and she ended up choosing a selection from a designer who was rela-

tively unknown at the time: The Lebanon-based Elie Saab, notable at that point for having dressed Queen Rania of Jordan. "I saw so many gowns, but this one just felt the part," she told the *Los Angeles Times*. "Classic, couture, modern, and sexy."

Her choice of words is pointed. The dress had to fill a part. It had to be cast in the role of Academy Award winner's dress just like any actor has to get cast in their award-winning role. If Berry was the lead, the gown was a supporting player.

It was everything she described. From the bottom down, it was luxurious, the fabric gathering around her ankles. The mesh burgundy top was indeed sexy, the embroidered flowers entwining over her torso, covering what needed to be covered, yet still leaving the illusion of nudity.

Berry is a woman who has constantly had to wrestle with her own sex appeal. She told *Variety* in 2020 that her looks have been both a blessing and a hurdle for her in Hollywood. "People always wanting to see my physical self first, and then some will argue, 'That's what got you in the door,'" she says. "But even if that got me in the door, I've had to fight that image of being stereotyped, fight to be seen as an artist."

In *Monster's Ball* she plays Leticia Musgrove, the wife of a man on death row (Sean Combs) who unwittingly starts up an affair with the racist prison guard (Billy Bob Thornton) responsible for the execution of her spouse. The movie is aggressively tragic. Horrible events pile up. It's both subtler than some might remember—it flirts with being a white savior narrative without actually being one—and just as blunt and clumsy as you might expect. Berry, who had broken out in Spike Lee's *Jungle Fever* and acted opposite Eddie Murphy in *Boomerang*, received effusive praise for her work. A.O. Scott wrote in the *New York Times* that she "proves herself to be an actress of impressive courage and insight." But the way in which she was sexualized immediately drew criticism. "The film's only flaw is the way Marc Forster allows his camera to linger on Berry's half-clothed beauty," Roger Ebert noted in his review.

At the center of *Monster's Ball* is a graphic, lengthy sex scene between Berry and Thornton's characters. She begs him to make her feel good after a night of drinking, during which they both discuss the deaths of their respective sons. That sex scene would continue to dog Berry.

Some months after Berry's win, Angela Bassett, an Oscar nominee for *What's Love Got to Do with It*, very publicly criticized the sexualized nature of Leticia in an interview with *Newsweek*. Bassett explained that she had turned down the part. "I couldn't do that because it's such a stereotype about black women and sexuality," she said. "Film is forever. It's about putting something out there you can be proud of 10 years later. I mean, Meryl Streep won Oscars without all that." Bassett wasn't the only person who argued that Leticia fed into the notion that Black women are overly sexual. In an editorial for the *Baltimore Sun*, writer Gregory Kane said that while Berry deserved her Oscar it was for a movie that was "silly and puerile." "Anybody notice the stereotype of the oversexed black woman coming into play here?" he wrote. "That hasn't been mentioned much. White commentators have steered clear of it. Blacks have discussed it only in private." Berry, for her part, has maintained that she believes that depicting sex was integral to Leticia's story: "I didn't feel it was exploitative. It was necessary for the character." She acknowledged the conversation again in an interview with the Guardian, pointing out a heightened standard when it came to her looks and her body. "A lot of things happen to people of color that don't happen to other people, and a lot of people don't realize it because they're not people of color," she said.

Berry's choice to wear something overtly sexy to the Oscars was an almost defiant stance. But it's also impossible to analyze her career that followed without thinking about how her perceived sexiness affected her work. At the time of her win, Berry was filming *Die Another Day*, playing Jinx, the latest Bond girl, a dubious honor more frequently bestowed at the time upon an up-and-comer than an Oscar-winning star. Opportunities came to her, but they were not with lauded directors and prestigious scripts. Before every single star was in a superhero movie, she made the play for her own franchise with *Catwoman* and instead became a joke. She now believes that the Oscar hurt her career rather than helped it. "I thought, 'Oh, all these great scripts are going to come my way; these great directors are going to be banging on my door.' It didn't happen," she told *Variety* in 2020. "It actually got a little harder. They call it the Oscar curse. You're expected to turn in award-worthy performances."

In choosing her gown, Berry anointed Saab as the next big thing in fashion. "Halle Berry made the name Elie Saab more popular," he later told *Vogue*. "She managed to really put the name Elie Saab on the international market." Via fashion Berry wielded her influence in full that night in 2002. She looked as glamorous and sexy as she wanted, and she started a trend many would follow. But leave it to Hollywood to turn that victory into something sour, to slowly rip that power away. Onstage, she paid tribute to "every nameless, faceless woman of color that now has a chance because this door tonight has been opened." She's still the only Black actress to ever win that prize.

michelle williams

(2006)

FOR MOST PEOPLE YELLOW IS A RISKY COLOR. IT CAN clash with so much. That's perhaps one of the reasons that Michelle Williams's Vera Wang gown continues to be cited as one of the best ever worn on the red carpet. Everything about the execution is both immaculate and surprising. The color—which has been described over the years as "saffron" and "mustard" and "canary"—is rich and warm, emphasized by her red lip. The cut is both classic, evoking bombshells of yore, and innovative, the lining around the breast feathering out as if she is a bird about to take flight.

That's an apt metaphor for Williams at this time in her career. She was only two years out from the end of *Dawson's Creek* and Jen Lindley, the role in the soapy teen drama that made her famous. In film, she had been slowly showing signs of the indie goddess she was about to become. Williams appeared in productions like *The Station Agent* as a sweet librarian, the role that ultimately led Ang Lee to cast her as Alma, the confused wife of Heath Ledger's Ennis Del Mar in *Brokeback Mountain*. Alma alerted audiences to the range of Williams's talents. Lee, in an interview with *Entertainment Weekly*, described her allure this way: "Something about her, you look at her and you wish her happiness. She's quite close to how Alma was written, this small beautiful woman with all that quality of vulnerability."

At the Oscars, Williams seemed to have achieved that happiness, the hue of her dress projecting sunniness above all else. Wang and Williams had reportedly worked closely on the custom design. She had reason to project happiness, and the viewers had reason to believe she was in a state of bliss. She had famously fallen in love with Heath Ledger on the set of *Brokeback*. Their daughter was born in late October 2005, just about a month before they would start to heavily promote the movie. Both Williams and Ledger—these young, attractive parents—were nominated for their first Oscars.

In the audience, watching Jon Stewart tell jokes, Ledger looked slightly uncomfortable, while Williams beamed. Neither of them would win their categories, but they were the night's golden couple.

What would ultimately follow is why it's hard to look at that yellow gown and not feel a pang of sadness. She and Ledger broke up. A year later he died of an accidental drug overdose. She, of course, would continue to do more spectacular work as an actress, earning three more Oscar nominations. But in the press her personal life would continue to be defined by the tragedy of losing Heath. Thirteen years later, she would tell *Vanity Fair* in a cover story that she "never gave up on love," explaining, "I always say to Matilda, 'Your dad loved me before anybody thought I was talented, or pretty, or had nice clothes.'" It's a statement that has a bit of self-mythologizing to it. Williams was the star of a wildly successful TV show before she met Ledger. But those words also conjure the image of Williams in that gown, beaming. "You look at her and you wish her happiness," Lee had said. Preserved in photography, bathed in gold, she is happiness incarnate.

pregnancy
at the oscars

TABLOID MEDIA IS WEIRD WHEN IT COMES TO PREGNANCY.
With few exceptions, when a celebrity gets pregnant, the realities of what is actually going on are glossed over in favor of reports on how the star in question is *glowing* as she *shows off* her *bump*. Five actresses have won Oscars while pregnant: Eva Marie Saint for *On the Waterfront* in 1955, Meryl Streep for *Sophie's Choice* in 1983, Catherine Zeta-Jones for *Chicago* in 2003, Rachel Weisz for *The Constant Gardener* in 2006, and finally Natalie Portman for *Black Swan* in 2012. More have attended the ceremony while carrying, both nominated and otherwise.

There is almost a uniform for the post-2000 pregnant winners, despite the range of designers they have gone to for gowns. Zeta-Jones, Weisz, and Portman all opted for empire waists, and off-the-shoulder bodices. The effect both emphasizes and hides the pregnancy at the same time. In close up, accepting their awards, they have the air of a Regency heroine.

All three of those women adhered to a strategy espoused by stylist Mary Alice Haney in an article about pregnancy at the Oscars for the *Hollywood Reporter*. "All tips to make you look thin apply doubly so when pregnant," she said. "Darker colors tend to be your friend, and a lot of ruffles or sequins are probably not the best when you're about to pop out a baby." That anyone should be concerned with looking skinny while incubating another human is nonsense, but that's Hollywood, baby.

Zeta-Jones was 10 days away from giving birth when she was the favorite to win for her wildly sexy performance as Velma Kelly in *Chicago*. While her costar, Renée Zellweger, opted out of performing the movie's nominated original song live because of stage fright, Zeta-Jones belted her heart out even as she "looked like she may have been on the verge of delivering her baby on stage," according to *Entertainment*

Weekly. In the custom black Versace frock, Zeta-Jones was described in one report as "ripe," in another as "magnificently pregnant." All these assessments were complimentary, sure, but also read as slightly uncomfortable with the fact of just *how* pregnant Zeta-Jones was. No matter the intent, it's weird to call a human being "ripe."

The press was even giddier about Natalie Portman's pregnant awards run. Portman was a former child star finally earning the Academy's seal of approval for her intense role as a ballerina going through a breakdown in Darren Aronofsky's film. By the time the Oscars rolled around she was engaged to Benjamin Millepied, the choreographer on *Black Swan*, and was pregnant with their child. News outlets frantically covered Portman's "pregnancy style" in the lead-up to her inevitable triumph. The *Los Angeles Times* gossip columnist "Ministry of Gossip," wrote that it "defies you to argue this award season hasn't been All. About. Natalie. Natalie Portman, that is." Portman ultimately wore a regal purple number from Rodarte, the brand that had designed the most ornate of *Black Swan*'s tutus. The neckline, once again, was the focus, jewel-encrusted and plunging toward a knot with fabric that fell over her stomach. *People* wrote that she "sported flushed cheeks," as if somehow that too was an accessory. On the red carpet, Portman reportedly said that "staying at home with messy hair in sweats is the biggest luxury of all." Maybe that's why when she was nominated for a second time while pregnant, for 2016's *Jackie*, she decided not to attend at all.

There's a reverence for the pregnant women who walk the red carpet at the Oscars, and a notion that they somehow embody the ideals of both maternity and traditional movie star beauty. But it's similarly telling that when the Academy was presented with an ad intended to air during the telecast about vagina cooling pads for postpartum moms, the institution deemed it too graphic. Pregnant women are allowed to look "ripe" when accepting their trophies, but get into the realities of childbirth? That's just too gross for the Oscars.

diablo cody

(2008)

BARRING THE OCCASIONAL SUPERCOOL COSTUME designer or musician nominated for Best Original Song, actors and actresses get the majority of the red carpet attention at the Oscars. It makes a grim sort of sense. Women don't often get nominated in categories outside of the gender-specific ones. As of publication, only seven women have been nominated for Best Director. Only two have actually won. The stats are a little better when it comes to the writing categories. Twenty women have won, but, until Emerald Fennell in 2021, the last time a woman triumphed in one of the two screenplay categories was in 2008, when Diablo Cody showed up in a free-flowing leopard-print Dior gown with a high slit, adding gold flats and a giant dangling skull earring. (A version of this essay was first published in 2018. It was incredibly disheartening to find that while there were women nominated for

writing in the interim, the number of winners still had changed so minimally.)

Cody wasn't just the rare woman to win a screenplay Oscar—she was the rare woman to come to the Oscars dressed as a raucous punk with visible tattoos and an attitude that said, "If you don't like me, tough luck." Few people, male and female, have ever been as much themselves at the award show, so Diablo was both celebrated and mercilessly mocked.

Diablo Cody, née Brook Busey-Hunt, emerged on the scene with a backstory that was almost as cinematic as the movie she wrote. Before she became a heralded screenwriter, she was a copy-typer-turned-stripper/blogger. Her blog yielded a memoir, *Candy Girl: A Year in the Life of an Unlikely Stripper*, which in turn yielded *Juno*, her film about a sardonic, talkative teen who gets pregnant after deciding to have sex with her best friend on a grody chair. The characters in *Juno* talked in Cody's own almost-too-clever dialect, spurting phrases like "home skillet" and "honest to blog." While the internet would later turn on her turns of phrase, when Cody emerged she was cool in a way that felt unusual for Hollywood. The site Jezebel, then in its nascency, showered her with praise. "If 'Jezebel' were a person, she very well might be up and coming screenwriter Diablo Cody, an ex-stripper and phone sex operator who pens hilarious movies with serious Oscar buzz, dresses like Courtney

Love did about halfway through her glam makeover (she wears satin jumpers but also combat boots), writes a blog called the *Pussy Ranch*, and has made it her mission to create films with multifaceted female leads. Diablo's heroines are not just reacting to the choices of male characters—these women are actually choosing their own destinies," the blogger who went by Jessica wrote.

Even before *Juno* was officially released, Cody had been deemed a sensation, anointed by Hollywood royalty like Steven Spielberg, who tapped her to write the pilot of a new Showtime series, *United States of Tara*. But as much as Diablo was an industry darling—one who wasn't afraid to call bullshit on the way women were treated in Hollywood—she was also on the defense. She got ahead of the well-trod notion that her work was "too stylized," telling *Entertainment Weekly*: "I've met so many hyperarticulate teenage girls who are not just shallow and image-obsessed." A profile by David Carr in the *New York Times* highlighted criticism from a Minneapolis-based writer who claimed that Diablo "wrote her own Wikipedia entry before living it." In all this good press there was also a sense that a backlash was coming, and come it did.

The Oscars gave her detractors a perfect time to pounce. When Cody showed up in that look, all of the people who were just waiting to call her out for her imagined transgressions had the perfect ammunition. "The diamond collar, the leopard print, the visible tattoos," Molly Friedman wrote at Gawker. "Kudos for daring Academy members to Take Notice and all, but an animal print dress will always be an animal print dress: tackiness exemplified." A writer over at Amoeba Music's blog of all places took issue with her tats. "I know this may make me unpopular, but as anyone who knows me knows, I firmly believe that tattoos (and chewing gum) have NO place on the red carpet on such a night as the Oscars," the scribe going by Miss Ess declared. "I mean, I know she was a stripper and all, but the Oscars are all about glamour, people. And leopard print, that's a whooooole other story."

Diablo did have her fans, including Dana Stevens at *Slate*, who applauded her boldness, while still couching her praise in the notion that Cody surpassed expectations. "As for Diablo Cody looking like a grown-up Pebbles Flintstone, I have a feeling she, too, would be delighted at the horror her outfit (a rhinestone-trimmed leopard-print muumuu slit to the hip, with skull-and-crossbones earrings and gold ballet flats) has provoked," Stevens argued. "I was all prepared to hate on Cody for being overpackaged and overconfident of her win, but she won my heart by showing up in a nutty getup clearly of her own devising and giving a speech that was unrehearsed, warm, and completely free of prefab Juno-esque zingers."

Cody was pretty explicit about the way she ended up onstage in leopard. She was assigned to blog about her experience at the Oscars for *EW* and described her fitting at Dior, writing: "I am shoehorned into a beautiful dress that evokes butterscotch, leopards, and Jesus. It is totally mega-swish." She explained that she wasn't allowed to dress herself anymore thanks to her newfound fame, but was clearly taken with this option, which, while styled, evoked what she wanted, which was to look "mega-swish."

Leopard print has a reputation, one that Diablo was capitalizing on when she chose to make it her signature. As Colette Shade once wrote on the website Racked, the pattern's history traverses high and low culture. When worn by the likes of Jackie O, Shade explained, leopard print can "evoke a kind of old-money femininity." But it is just as easily "a signal of poor taste and of 'trashiness,' which really means that it represents the sexually available lower-class woman." Diablo was successfully embracing both sides of leopard at the Oscars: She was at the fanciest event imaginable, yet slyly winking at her semi-sordid past—one she was proud to flaunt.

Almost immediately following the ceremony, Diablo was beset by twin controversies that, when combined, say a lot. First: her shoes. Word emerged that she elected to wear those flats over a pair of $1 million Stuart Weitzman heels she had initially selected. This was deemed ungrateful in the blogosphere. In a MySpace post about the switch, Diablo explained that she had signed up to don the designer footwear without realizing it was a publicity stunt for the brand. "This looks really attention-whorey, and for once, I didn't do it on purpose," she wrote. Jezebel's Dodai Stewart, defending Diablo, pointed out the vitriol over on the blog Oh No They Didn't! where readers wrote comments like, "Uh, you're a stripper/screenwriter. Whoring out should not be a problem for you," and called her a "cunt."

But that wasn't even the worst of it. Almost immediately following Diablo's win, a website called Egotastic leaked nude photos of her. And because she used to strip, the consensus among some publications was simply: Take a look! Bloggers even seemed to take the fact that she wore a leopard-print dress as permission to provide leering commentary. "After all, one glance at her proudly displayed tattoo and that Oscar dress she was wearing (which she so demurely held with her free hand so as to not give America an internationally broadcast upskirt), and you know she had to be one hell of an exotic dancer," Kevin Carr speculated in a now deleted post at Film School Rejects.

Since Diablo's Oscar run in 2007, the public conversation around women, their bodies, and their place in the industry has both evolved and remained frustratingly stagnant. It's hard to imagine that outlets today would celebrate the leak of nudes rather than condemning such an action for the massive violation it is. On the other hand, the system Cody was intent on disrupting is still very much in place. She told *EW* way back when that she felt a "responsibility" to try to direct because "there's such a paucity of female directors." Ten years later, Diablo's point still very much stands. (Her own directorial debut, *Paradise*, floundered, but as she said, "There are worse things you can do in life than direct a bad movie.")

In general, loud women are frowned upon. And Diablo Cody was a loud woman with a loud style that she wasn't going to change just because writers are supposed to blend into the background, typing in solitude in darkened rooms. Leopard print isn't what you're supposed to wear to the Oscars, but where would we be if women did only what they were supposed to?

gabourey sidibe

(2010)

THE FIRST PROFILES WRITTEN ABOUT GABOUREY Sidibe were all pretty much centered around one thing: The 20-something from Harlem was not actually the abused teenager she played in the movie that made her famous. A *New York Times* story from 2007—two years before *Precious: Based on the Novel Push by Sapphire*, would hit theaters and garner Sidibe her Oscar nomination—was explicit: "Desk-job ambitions or not, Gabourey Sidibe is not Precious; she is a natural performer." A *Guardian* piece took it even further, opening, "Just for the record, Gabby Sidibe is not a functionally illiterate high-school girl." It seemed like no matter how often it was stated for the record, members of the media had a hard time believing this truth.

Expressing a personal connection to a character can make for a better narrative—especially in the press-heavy lead-up to an Oscar contender's release. The audience always searches for authenticity, and Sidibe's Precious seemed to provide that. Roger Ebert wrote of the film, "[She] so completely creates the Precious character that you rather wonder if she's very much like her." In the film, she wears the pain of her character in her eyes and on her shoulders, and to some it appeared too visceral to not have been lived. But if you follow her on Twitter, you know that Sidibe is one of the funniest people around. She isn't Precious. And yet the media seemed to wish she were, because off-screen she didn't easily fit inside the boxes of the Oscar-industrial complex.

On the festival circuit for Precious, Sidibe wasn't treated like other young starlets. She explains in her memoir This Is Just My Face: Try Not to Stare that she didn't have money for a stylist, so she shopped for herself—buying prom dresses from plus-size boutique Torrid to wear at Sundance and Cannes. Even in the four months between those festivals—after the film had already won widespread acclaim and awards—no one told her that she'd need to wear fancy attire. "I was told that the dress code was 'casual,'" she writes. "That was a lie." She wore jeans under a paisley frock to Cannes, while her costars Mariah Carey and Paula Patton were outfitted in cocktail dresses.

By the time awards season rolled around, the movie's distributor Lionsgate would set Sidibe up with a stylist named Linda Medvene. They weren't a great match. Sidibe didn't feel comfortable telling Medvene whose style she actually wanted to imitate—Kim Parker, the character from *Moesha*—so she just told her, "I don't need a dress that will stand out. I'll do that anyway. I just want to look like I belong." What followed was continued media skepticism about just how Gabby, as a plus-size woman, would look on the Oscars' red carpet, with headlines like "Gabourey Sidibe's Dress Mystery: When Plus Size Is Too Big for Hollywood" and "Gabby's Red Carpet Presence Sparks Plus-Size Debate." Others were less explicit but no less uncomfortable. "What Will the Best-Actress Nominees Wear on Oscar Night?" asked *Vanity Fair*. "A woman with curves, Sidibe has been choosing empire-waist gowns, and this Marchesa dress fits the bill," they surmised, putting a photo of the actress side by side with a runway look featuring off-the-shoulder ruffles. "The detail at the neckline extends over the tops of the arms, a problem area for some women, and bright white would really pop against her complexion." Phrases like "problem area" and "complexion" dance around Gabby's weight and race but are no less insidious.

Medvene, meanwhile, was using Sidibe as a prop to promote her work and to show off how tolerant she was of people who didn't look like the typical Hollywood clients. In February of that year, Medvene spoke to *USA Today* and announced that Marchesa—the brand founded by Harvey Weinstein's then-wife

Georgina Chapman—was dressing Sidibe, insisting that her size wouldn't be a hindrance in finding a gown by such a high-profile designer. "We've been offered dresses by all these huge designers. It just proves that anyone can dress a full-sized woman," Medvene said. "Working with Gabby has been so easy because she's so comfortable with who she is, in her skin."

But just two days before the ceremony, in an interview with Fox, Medvene confusingly said that Marchesa wasn't actually going to be responsible for Sidibe's dress. Fox was running a feature that asked why Gabby hadn't "been given the same star-studded styling treatment" as Jennifer Hudson a couple years prior—implying, essentially, that Gabby was just too plus-size for the industry. While ostensibly written to call out Hollywood, the article largely featured experts hiding behind anonymity and using coded language to frame Sidibe as an outsider. One nameless boutique owner said, "I hate to say that, because she seems like such an amazing person, but she doesn't 'fit' who they design for."

Meanwhile Medvene's strange behavior didn't go unnoticed at the time. Erica Kennedy, writing in *Salon*, declared, "This is some reeeeal funny style bullshit going on here and my only consolation is to believe that Gabby is so above and beyond this surface CRAP that hopefully it will not affect her or let it ruin her night."

Weirdly, Sidibe did end up wearing Marchesa. The actress showed up in a rich blue gown, draped with a Grecian air and embellished with silver floral embroidery that matched the jewels in her bracelet, ring, and hair. The red carpet watchers approved. Heather Cocks at Go Fug Yourself raved, "I love that this dress suits her better than anything I've seen her in so far—great color, cool detail, and a simple style that accentuates the right things." *Teen Vogue* listed her as one of the 10 best dressed at the event, writing: "Gabourey looked like a red-carpet queen in a regal blue Marchesa dress with perfectly coiffed hair and loads of diamonds." On the red carpet, at least, Gabby triumphed.

During the ceremony, Sidibe lost Best Actress to Sandra Bullock in *The Blind Side*, a movie that used a large Black actor as a prop to convey how sympathetic Bullock's white Southern mom was. As for Sidibe, the media quickly continued publishing stories questioning her weight and future in the business. Just days after the Oscars in March 2010, CNN asked, "Can Talent Outweigh Size in Hollywood?" The piece cites Howard Stern, who claimed on his radio show that Gabby's "never going to be in another movie." (Not true.) A blog post at SFGate countered that the bigger issue was racism: "Gabourey Sidibe Isn't Too Fat for Hollywood, She's Too Black." By the end of the month, Jezebel insisted, "Enough About Sidibe's Weight, Already."

More than ten years out from her Oscar nomination, Sidibe seems to be, frankly, living her best life. She's been a series regular on multiple TV shows. She's engaged. She's going to direct her first film. She wears bold prints in bright colors. But *Precious* still occasionally looms over her career and her life. In *This Is Just My Face,* Gabby described how during Halloween 2016, friends sent her photos of people dressed up as the character Precious. She's not offended by the costumes, but rather by the pals who want her to laugh at the photos with them. "We may have the same face and body, but we stand for two completely different things," Sidibe wrote. "Precious is a survivor, and I refuse to be anyone's survivor because I prefer to think of myself as a winner."

anne hathaway

(2013)

ANNE HATHAWAY WAS THE FRONT-RUNNER ON OSCAR night 2013, but, even if she claimed the trophy, there was no way she was ever going to win in the public eye. Hathaway's status as a punching bag was sealed the moment she stepped onto the red carpet at the Dolby Theatre. A dress wasn't going to change that, but a dress could make it worse. And it did.

Looking back on it all, the vitriol directed Hathaway's way during the 2012–13 Oscar season was nothing short of shameful in what otherwise should have been a fantastic year for the actress. She had two big blockbusters coming out: *The Dark Knight Rises*, in which she played Catwoman, and *Les Misérables*, for which she almost immediately won critical acclaim for her ragged solo, "I Dreamed a Dream."

But affection for Hathaway curdled the more she appeared in public. At the beginning of December—*Les Mis* was sched-

uled to hit on Christmas—BuzzFeed published a post asking, "Why Do People Hate Anne Hathaway?" It wasn't a rigorous investigation (obviously), just a collection of tweets from random users who assert that she "ruins everything" among other non-offenses like having a face. In February the next year, writer Brian Moylan tried to get to the bottom of "Hathahate" with a reported piece for Hollywood.com. His conclusion: She was too much of a "theatre kid," eager to please, trying too hard to be "likable," whatever that means.

Disliking Anne Hathaway during these months was treated as something of a sport. Even I joined in: I wrote a post for my employer at the time, the *Atlantic Wire*, predicting just how annoying she would be on Oscar night. She swept the precursor awards, and every subsequent appearance added more fuel to the fire. Her jokes were seen as hokey, and her surprise at her now expected triumphs was perceived as disingenuous. At the Golden Globes she said, "blergh," a faux goofy exclamation that she credited to host Tina Fey who popularized it on *30 Rock*.

By the time February 24 rolled around, Hathaway was facing an army of Twitter critics who would despise her no matter what she did. And her choice of garment only exacerbated their vitriol. Early in the evening the fashion house Valentino sent out a press release stating that she would be wearing one of its dresses, described as a "a pink embroidered tulle illusion gown." Instead, she showed up in a pastel pink Prada, soft in color, but severe in style, angular in all the wrong places. The boatneck evoked Audrey Hepburn's 1954 dress, but the fabric seemed stiff. And worst of all it looked very much like her nipples were showing through the fabric, even though that was just the way the garment was constructed. She was doomed.

Novelty Twitter accounts were still popular—and not quite so lame—in 2013 so, within minutes of her appearance, @HathawayNipple cropped up. Its inaugural tweet? "Anyone else feeling a little chilly?" Hathaway smiled through it. She confessed to E! that the gown was a last minute pick, but she liked how it made her feel her age: "I tried on a ton of dresses and, at the end of the day, I loved the simplicity of it. And this sounds weird, but I'm 30 and I feel 30 in this, and that's a very positive thing."

Hathaway's way of framing her choice—like most of what Hathaway does—was a smart bit of self-evaluation. As a performer she was constantly striving for a maturity not often afforded to her. Oscar night 2013 was the peak of her career. She wanted to look and feel like the woman she had grown into.

She rose to fame as a teen queen in *The Princess Diaries*, an endlessly rewatchable movie that established not just her wide-grinned charm but also her comedic chops. But she did not want to get trapped in the Disney bubble that had caught so many of her peers. In 2005 she appeared in the one-two punch of *Havoc*—an edgy but poorly received teen drama— and *Brokeback Mountain*, the lauded phenomenon. Both roles put her in dark, adult situations where she didn't have to be Mia Thermopolis-adjacent anymore. *Les Mis* wasn't even her first acting nomination: She was honored back in 2008 for playing a recovering addict in *Rachel Getting Married*.

Where did it go wrong for Anne Hathaway? You can probably blame the Oscars for that as well. For the ceremony honoring the 2010 movie season in 2011, producers Bruce Cohen and Don Mischer wanted to appeal to a younger audience, so instead of hiring a seasoned comedian to host they went for two popular, attractive actors: Hathaway and James Franco. The night was a disaster. Franco seemed uninterested or possibly high. Hathaway did her darndest to keep the show afloat, but she seemed to be flailing. In the aftermath of the fiasco, Franco leaned further into his intellectual schtick, getting to make whatever Faulkner adaptations he wished, but that night haunted Hathaway. Memories of her desperation followed her all the way back to the Dolby. Once again, the story goes, she was trying too hard.

When her name was called and she was handed her hard-won trophy in 2013, she looked at it and declared, "It came true." The line—a reference to her own dreams and the fact that she won for singing a song about dreams—was immediately viewed as smug. It wasn't *cool* for her to admit that she'd chased a goal and was happy that she finally achieved it.

In the days following the Oscars, various websites were flooded with think pieces trying to figure out just *why* so many people detest her. "I can't figure out why I don't like Anne Hathaway. Or rather, why we don't," Ann Friedman wrote in *The Cut*. On top of that, her dress scandal wouldn't seem to go away. Her choice was interpreted as another ding on her character. Her costar Amanda Seyfried turned up in a frock that was similar to the Valentino Hathaway was supposed to wear, so Hathaway's swap was seen as a competitive maneuver that somehow also betrayed a friend who was loyal to her: Valentino himself, who had designed her wedding dress. The Valentino in question was less rigid, more like what the public wants from a starlet: a high neck melting into a flowing skirt. It was, yes, similar to the Armani Privé that Seyfried wore, but also akin to the Dior Jennifer Lawrence would wear while winning best actress, tripping on her way up to collect her trophy (see page 64).

Ultimately, two days after the party, Hathaway came out with an apology: "It came to my attention late Saturday night that there would be a dress worn to the Oscars that is remarkably similar to the Valentino I had intended to wear, and so I decided it was best for all involved to change my plans. Though

I love the dress I did wear, it was a difficult last-minute decision as I had so looked forward to wearing Valentino in honor of the deep and meaningful relationship I have enjoyed with the house and with Valentino himself. I deeply regret any disappointment caused."

The statement is grim. Hathaway should have been coasting on joy but instead was forced to publicly grovel. The apology is almost an admission of defeat: Fine, Twitter masses, you won.

It's easy to look back on the Hathahate as one part of a wildly sexist Oscars where host Seth MacFarlane sang a song about seeing actresses' boobs and a tweet from the *Onion* called nine-year-old nominee Quvenzhané Wallis the c-word. But it's also easy to forget how hating Anne Hathaway passed for a pop culture commentary during that moment.

Hathaway is seemingly doing just fine. When she reemerged on the press circuit, she was outspoken about the flogging she endured without seeming bitter about it—although that good humor is likely another trick of the trade to ward off more venom. She opted for weirder, bigger, and bolder projects. She seemed to be having fun. She won the internet over again. But it's important to remember: She never did anything that warranted her losing its love in the first place.

lupita nyong'o

(2014)

L UPITA NYONG'O'S PRADA GOWN WAS NOT JUST BLUE. It was not simply baby blue or powder blue either. According to the actress herself, it was "Nairobi blue," an ode to her hometown in Kenya. "It's a blue that reminds me of Nairobi, so I wanted to have a little bit of home," she told Ryan Seacrest on the red carpet. The Prada was both timeless and thoroughly distinctive, custom-made for a star to whom those same adjectives could easily be applied.

Nyong'o's ascent to fashion and Hollywood icon status during the 2013–14 awards season was one of the quickest rises in recent memory. When she was cast in Steve McQueen's *12 Years a Slave*, she hadn't yet appeared in a single feature film. Her most notable previous on-screen role was in the African television series *Shuga*. But from the time *12 Years* premiered at the Toronto International Film Festival in September 2013 to March of the following year, Nyong'o was unstoppable.

Shortly after the movie debuted, Vulture awards writer Kyle Buchanan declared that it would win Best Picture. Nyong'o was mentioned in a parenthetical. While the other actors in the film were delivering some of their best work, Nyong'o stood out as a "surefire Supporting Actress nominee . . . building a career on the spot." A recent graduate of the Yale School of Drama, McQueen picked Nyong'o to play Patsey, a slave who is brutally raped and abused over the course of the film, which was adapted from the memoir of Solomon Northup, a free man tricked and sold into slavery in 1841. Patsey is the vessel through which Northup, portrayed by Chiwetel Ejiofor, and the audience experience the most upsetting horrors of slavery.

Nyong'o started winning immediate acclaim for her sense of style. She took the business of being a fashion star just as seriously as she took her work acting. She linked up with the stylist Micaela Erlanger through her friend, actress Michelle Dockery. She treated being a style icon as a job the same way she would treat any part. "When I knew I was going to be doing the press tour for *12 Years A Slave*, I got to work and started researching what was happening in the formal world of fashion to try and articulate to myself what my style would be in it all," she told the *Daily Beast*. "It's been a great education—a great discovery—to find clothing artists who are doing things that I feel express something about myself. And there are so many."

The praise for both Nyong'o's performance and her ability to dominate a fashion event was swift. Days after *12 Years a Slave* was released in the United States, the *New York Times* declared that she "impresses on the red carpet," with the note that she "has been quick to attract the attention of top designers looking to dress the Next Big Thing."

It's not unusual that a young Oscar contender (man or woman) becomes a phenomenon for both their work and appearance, but with Nyong'o it was impossible not to acknowledge that her undeniable beauty was rare for Hollywood. Not only was she a Black actress, but she was a dark-skinned Black actress. And as racist as both the entertainment and fashion industries are, they are equally colorist, elevating lighter-skinned people of color if they choose to diversify at all.

Nyong'o, born in Mexico and raised in Kenya, addressed this head-on. In an incredibly moving speech delivered upon receiving the award for Best Breakthrough Performance at the Essence Awards the February before the Academy Awards, Nyong'o spoke extensively about the self-hatred she experienced because of the darkness of her skin. She described how revolutionary it was for her to see model Alek Wek, who has a similar skin tone, celebrated. "My complexion had always been an obstacle to overcome and all of a sudden Oprah was telling me it wasn't," she said. "It was perplexing, and I wanted to reject it because I had begun to enjoy the seduction of inadequacy. But a flower couldn't help but bloom inside of me, when I saw Alek, I inadvertently saw a reflection of myself that I could not deny. Now, I had a spring in my step because I felt more seen, more appreciated by the far away gatekeepers of beauty." Nyong'o knew the impact her very presence on magazine covers and in makeup campaigns would have. She was named *People*'s Most Beautiful Woman and became the face of Lancôme. She was labeled, like so many before her, an "It" girl. Which is not to say her beauty was consistently celebrated or that certain powerful entities didn't attempt to morph it. *Vanity Fair* was accused of lightening her skin in its "Vanities" feature. Her omnipresence was debated. Some argued that she was being exoticized or oversaturated; that she was being praised for a performance that perpetuated the notion that Hollywood only likes stories of Black suffering. Dodai Stewart, writing for Jezebel, countered that there was no such thing as too much Lupita. "Her face everywhere helps us, as a society, on our journey as we come to terms with recognizing and embracing non-Caucasian beauty," she wrote. "Visibility is key."

At every ceremony in the lead-up to the Oscars, Nyong'o wore a magnificent gown, always opting for bold colors: red at the Golden Globes; teal at the SAGs. Leading up to the Academy Awards, set for the beginning of March, one of the biggest questions was what she would wear. The Nairobi blue was softer than the other shades she had chosen. She kept twirling, the skirt like a cloud around her. It was a moment designed for the history books. And it achieved that status. From then on she would be forever inscribed in the best dressed lists.

In the immediate years following her Oscar win, Nyong'o was in high-profile movies, but her face was not seen on-screen. Her character in *Star Wars* was an alien creature. In *The Jungle Book*, she was a wolf. Fans started to wonder if all of the celebration that followed her that Oscar season was hollow. She didn't have a starring role in front of the camera until 2016's *Queen of Katwe*. That concern has since dissipated with her roles in *Black Panther* and *Us*, though even in a leading on-screen role she still knows the power of her image, specifically the image of her in that blue.

In the children's book she wrote titled *Sulwe* the eponymous heroine wears that same blue, a choice by illustrator Vashti Harrison. "Vashti chose to put her in a dress color similar to the one I wore to my first #Oscars in 2014. It was a night that dreams are made of, beyond my imagination," Nyong'o wrote on Instagram. "With Sulwe, I wanted to give dark skin permission to exist in the world of dreams and imagination, where possibilities and potential really grow." For Nyong'o the Nairobi blue represents dreams come true. It will for countless others as well.

zendaya

(2015)

ENDAYA WAS NOT THE GALACTIC CELEBRITY SHE IS now when she arrived on the Oscars red carpet in 2015. She had just launched her second Disney Channel series, *K.C. Undercover*. Occasionally, websites affixed her surname "Coleman" to her moniker or called her a "pop star." She wasn't in any of the nominated movies. In fact, she hadn't yet appeared on-screen in a single movie herself. That wouldn't happen until she was in *Spider-Man: Homecoming* two years later. But all of her future success can easily be tied back to February 2015. It wasn't just that she looked gorgeous. (Of course, she did.) It was everything that followed.

The event was something of a coming out party for Zendaya. She was there to claim her place in the Hollywood ecosystem, and she and her longtime stylist Law Roach, who operated a vintage store in Chicago before closing it to work with her, were exacting about their inspirations for her look. It was a mix of classic Hollywood glamour with a modern bent. The dress was Vivienne Westwood, a little bit screen siren, a little bit Greek deity. The hair: pure Lisa Bonet. Zendaya posted a side by side of her profile alongside the actress best known for *A Different World* and *High Fidelity*. She and Roach knew they were doing something radical, pairing locs, an ode to one of the icons of '90s cool, with the sleek Westwood. In the story accompanying Zendaya's first *Vogue* cover, published two years later, writer Abby Aguirre explained that Roach creates characters for each appearance. This one was "Dreadlocks Goddess."

The fashion bible immediately crowned her the "breakout style star" of these Academy Awards. In the accompanying piece, Alessandra Codinha declared: "If you didn't know who Zendaya was before tuning into the 87th Annual Academy Awards tonight, well, you will now: The lissome and lovely Disney actress and pop singer caused a stir on the red carpet in a figure-hugging ivory-toned Vivienne Westwood slip of a goddess gown, replete with flowing dreadlocks: one part Lisa Bonet, one part Venus de Milo, and all very grown up (which is to say, all very un-Disney)."

But her moment soon curdled. On the post-ceremony episode of *Fashion Police*, host Giuliana Rancic, the presenter who has taken over for Joan Rivers as perhaps the primary gadfly of carpet culture, gazed at a picture of Zendaya's locs and remarked that they "overwhelmed her" and that she smelled like "patchouli oil . . . or weed."

The condemnation of Rancic's comments was, appropriately, swift. In her effort to make a casually snarky comment about fashion, she had directed racist invective toward someone who was still a teenager, associating a traditionally Black hairstyle with drugs and undesirable smells. There were plenty of responses to Rancic, but none more impactful than the one that came from Zendaya herself, which she posted on her social media. She wrote that her father, brother, best childhood friend, and little cousins all have locs. She cited Ava DuVernay, whose film *Selma* had been nominated for Best Picture that year, as also having locs, as well as singer-songwriter Ledisi, and Harvard professor Vincent Brown. She said: "There is already harsh criticism of African American hair in society without the help of ignorant people who choose to judge others based on the curl of their hair. My wearing my hair in locs on an Oscar red carpet was to showcase them in a positive light, to remind people of color that our hair is good enough."

Rancic scrambled to come up with a worthy apology, at first in a tweet and then on TV, all while trying to maintain that the clip was edited to leave out the mention of her talking about hippies. Her comments may have been rooted in ignorance rather than malice, but the crack spoke to the larger, often toxic, culture of whiteness that orbits the Oscars.

Zendaya was hardly the first person to wear locs to the

Oscars. Past host and winner Whoopi Goldberg had worn her trademark hairstyle to the ceremony multiple times before. Zendaya wasn't even the only person to wear her hair in locs on the 2015 carpet. DuVernay, whom the young performer had noted in her statement, kept her locs while also sporting an updo for the awards show.

But DuVernay was also representative of how the Oscars had failed when it came to supporting Black artists. That very same year April Reign created the hashtag #OscarsSoWhite to highlight how the Academy was routinely ignoring the work of creators of color. *Selma*, though almost universally praised by critics, was snubbed in nearly all major categories save for Best Picture. All the acting nominees were white. DuVernay was passed over for a Best Director nomination.

Zendaya walked into this hostile climate. In a less-discussed moment from the *Fashion Police* episode, Kathy Griffin made a crack about not knowing who she was or why she was there. That was, in a way, an understandable, though uneducated statement. Unless you were following the Disney Channel, you likely wouldn't have known that this 18-year-old was a producer of her own show, demanding that it depict a family of color and show that girls don't have to sing and dance to be deemed worthy by society. Griffin and her fellow commentators did not know that soon Zendaya would become the youngest person ever to win the Emmy for Outstanding Lead Actress in a Drama Series—an accomplishment she achieved just five years later. But everyone underestimated Zendaya at their own peril. Not only did she establish herself as a Gen Z style icon that very day, she also met callous, curt commentary with a thoughtful condemnation of the inherent racism that she and so many other Black stars face on a daily basis.

This was just the beginning of Zendaya's moment. I fully believe she'll be back at the Oscars as a nominee, and in the meantime she'll continue shaping an unfair business in her own image.

in memoriam
the mani cam

WAS E!'S MANI CAM AN INNOCUOUS TOY? A HEINOUS affront to feminism? Just sort of stupid? For three years it terrorized the stars attending shows like the Oscars, the Emmys, and the Grammys, until it became a loathed focal point in the dialogue around red carpet mores and then, finally, disappeared.

What exactly was the Mani Cam? Well, to put it simply, it was a camera for manicures. The E! crew built a mini red carpet for stars to walk their fingers down, thereby showing off the work of their manicurists and whatever exorbitant jewels happened to be adorning their hands. It's not, inherently, a terrible idea. Nail art has only become more popular in recent years, and the people who make that happen deserve to have their talents on display.

But the pageantry of it was inherently ridiculous. And stars revolted. Jennifer Lawrence, famously, stuck her face in it on the night she won her Oscar, yelling at her friend (soon to be Oscar winner) Emma Stone: "Your ass is mine, Stone." The camera wasn't even plugged in, so they didn't get the shot. And there was an unspoken hierarchy to who was chosen for the Mani Cam. When Catherine Zeta-Jones appeared to actually want to partake in the fun, Ryan Seacrest ignored her.

Soon, celebrities started just outright refusing. Julianne Moore, who rejected the Mani Cam at the SAG Awards, described it as "humiliating" in 2015. Moore's distaste for the Mani Cam heralded its end, which coincided with the #AskHerMore movement.

There's nothing wrong with a woman showing off her fingers if she wants to, but forcing her to do so crosses a line. In the Mani Cam we find a microcosm of all the contradictions of the Oscars' red carpet and the focus on fashion. Fashion can be a means of expression, but it can also be a prison. The Mani Cam was the latter.

jenny beavan

(2016)

THE VIRAL VIDEO SUPPOSEDLY SAID IT ALL. COSTUME designer Jenny Beavan walked down the Dolby Theatre's aisle to collect her trophy for *Mad Max: Fury Road* while besuited men looked at her sternly. The clip, posted by *Entertainment Weekly* writer Dalton Ross, set off a sandstorm of media coverage as vicious as the arid land Furiosa drove through in George Miller's action film. The initial consensus was clear: It seemed like these men, including best director nominees Tom McCarthy and Alejandro González Iñárritu, were not clapping for Beavan because she had the audacity to show up to the Oscars wearing a bedazzled pleather jacket, black trousers, and sensible shoes.

That was not exactly true. The snippet caught a brief moment when the crowd was not applauding Beavan. Iñárritu even released a statement to clear his name, explaining that he only felt "admiration" for Beavan and her work, and: "I've

learned a lot this awards season . . . that I should never cross my arms when I am sitting down."

For as much as the outrage was directed at Iñárritu and his ilk, the controversy that surrounded Beavan's outfit said more about the media, feminist and otherwise, and how unbelievable it was that a woman would skirt tradition so drastically and show up dressed casually at an event where being fancy is all but required.

Beavan interpreted the dress code at the Oscars as implied rather than stated. "I think it may have said to wear black tie, but you know nothing about whether you must wear heels, not like in Cannes where apparently any woman who walks down the red carpet has to wear heels," she wrote in an essay for the *Hollywood Reporter* after the fracas. It's not like Beavan wasn't well aware of what was expected of her when she arrived in 2016. *Mad Max: Fury Road* marked her 10th nomination and second win. Her first was all the way back in 1987 for the Merchant Ivory film *A Room with a View*. Back then she wore a spin on a tux with a bow tie and an untucked shirt, her trademark scarf still around her neck.

It would be a mistake to think that Beavan's 2016 look wasn't carefully considered. She's a costume designer after all. She saw the outfit as a tip of the proverbial hat to the movie for which she was nominated, a dystopian opera of cars and skulls. The image on the back of her jacket was the head of *Fury Road*'s villain, Immortan Joe. She told the *Guardian* she wanted her scarf to look like an "oily rag." She painted one nail silver, in tribute to Immortan Joe's blessing, "you will ride eternal shiny and chrome." It was designed for both comfort and recognition of her own work and that of George Miller. "The thing that lots of people are missing is that I was wearing a costume," she said in the *Guardian* interview. "An homage to Mad Max. I look ridiculous in frocks. I can't wear heels—my back goes out and my feet get terribly sore. And besides, I have no interest in clothes other than what they tell me about a person. I am a storyteller—I'm not interested in fashion. Other than people like Alexander McQueen. The rest of it is just so much Cinderella stuff." (It's worth mentioning that she assesses her style with a large dose of self-deprecation, telling *THR*: "It will always be trousers, because there is absolutely no way I would frighten the L.A. natives with my legs.")

Costume designers are often some of the most nontraditionally dressed people at the awards. Lizzy Gardiner, who won in 1995 for her work on *Priscilla, Queen of the Desert*, came in a golden frock made of old American Express cards. In 2020, legendary designer Sandy Powell, nominated for her work on *The Irishman*, showed up in a white, bell-bottomed suit that had been signed by her fellow nominees. Ruth E. Carter, who became the first Black person to ever win the award in 2019 for *Black Panther*, wore a shimmering, dramatic gown, with a jeweled collar that echoed the Wakandan fashion she had created. Beavan knew she looked out of place, but she also knew exactly what she was doing.

The chatter about Beavan's awards show appearances had started even before the Oscars. At the BAFTAs a week earlier, comedian Stephen Fry joked that she was a "bag lady," and was met with such outrage that he left Twitter. Beavan wasn't bothered. Fry is a friend of hers. But the internet was incredibly mad on her behalf.

It was a cycle that repeated itself after the Oscars clip spread. The public misinterpreted the reaction to Beavan as anti-feminist and took a stand. In the *Toronto Star*, columnist Heather Mallick argued that Iñárritu "looked repelled," and that "The Men of the Oscars disliked Beavan for not being a damp gamine in a gown." But in retrospect it is almost as if the anger itself also came from a place of squeamishness. In the pile-on to defend Beavan—who didn't care—it was as if the defenders were tripping over themselves to show how okay they were with a woman who didn't conform to the norms of Oscar fashion. It's difficult to deduce whether some of the people who were gazing upon her were actually taking umbrage at her appearance. It's possible that some of the glances were just of confusion. No matter how you slice it, Beavan looked out of place at the Oscars, the same way Frances McDormand did when she wore a denim jacket to the Tonys. It's a formal event and Beavan did not dress formally.

By being comfortable, Jenny Beavan made people uncomfortable. She was not ignorant, even if she may not have been perturbed by any of the uproar. Beavan's entire job is to think about clothes and what they represent. She attended the awards knowing there was a chance her outfit would be broadcast to the world. Instead of conforming to the standards of the Oscars, she decided she would conform to the standards of both her own personal style and the movie she was there to represent. In this case that meant evoking a toxic wasteland where oil is currency and a motorcycle jacket is really the only option.

men
at the oscars

WAS 2018 THE YEAR MEN STARTED DRESSING WITH INTENT at the Oscars? It was at least a turning point, and now we're never going back to the days of boring male homogeny. Why 2018? In 2018, Adam Rippon wore a harness. Chadwick Boseman wore a long black coat with silver embroidered shoulders. Both men were celebrated for their risky choices. From there the floodgates opened. The next year, Billy Porter wore a velvet tuxedo gown. Jason Momoa also went for velvet—pink velvet. Mahershala Ali wore a black beanie and oversized glasses. Spike Lee appeared in purple. Boseman even upped his game further, with beaded tails. Finally, men were taking risks in their attire and showing their personalities in the same way women have been doing for years. And instead of being mocked, they were celebrated.

It's not as if all men prior to 2018 wore boring tuxes. There were always the outliers. In 1968, Sammy Davis Jr. wore a suit with a high collar and a beaded lapel to accept the award for Best Original Song on behalf of Leslie Bricusse. Dudes looked dashing, certainly. The likes of Sidney Poitier and Steve McQueen, two of the coolest actors ever, opted for tails. When Jack Nicholson won his first award in 1976 for *One Flew Over the Cuckoo's Nest*, he sat through the ceremony wearing his signature sunglasses, only taking them off when he actually stood up to get his trophy.

Until the 2010s, when guys took red carpet risks—especially when they challenged gender norms—they frequently landed on "worst dressed" lists. In *GQ*'s catalogue of the "worst-dressed men of all-time" Robert Downey Jr. was lambasted for trying bows instead of ties. Will Smith, Russell Crowe, and Samuel L. Jackson were mocked for going for overcoats instead of suit jackets. I won't defend the styling entirely, but there was a distinct sense that if a man opted for anything but a traditional tux at the Oscars, he was disobeying some unspoken rule.

ADAM RIPPON'S HARNESS

Every so often the Academy invites stars of the moment to the party, and in 2018 Adam Rippon was one of the most talked about people on the planet. He had just won a bronze medal as part of the Olympic team competing in South Korea and had made international headlines for being the first openly gay athlete to be part of the U.S. Olympic team at the Winter Games. Though that arguably should not have been such a landmark in 2018, Rippon was out and loud about it on a global stage, standing among representatives from countries with anti-LGBTQ+ laws, as the U.S. administration was simultaneously attempting to strip away protections for gay people.

And then he showed up to the Oscars in a leather harness. He stood on the red carpet with his hands at the waist of his jacket with tails drawing attention to the halter, which was affixed to his body where a vest would otherwise be. The daring look was designed by Jeremy Scott of Moschino. It was sexy and suggestive. Rippon, typically, was unapologetic about his choice, which was largely cheered by fashion critics. "I think fashion is all about self-expression and I chose to wear what I wore on the red carpet because I felt cool AF. Everyone should take risks, be bold, and not give a [poop emoji]," Rippon wrote on Twitter.

Together, Scott and Rippon took an item associated with BDSM in the gay community, more likely to be seen in the Folsom Street Fair than the Academy Awards, and put it on the most mainstream platform there is. This was not the kind of LGBTQ+ culture that was intended to be palatable for heterosexual, cisgender viewers. It was pure and unabashed.

From there the harness took off. The next year, Timothée Chalamet wore one to the Golden Globes and Michael B. Jordan wore one to the SAG Awards. Both were softer in style than Rippon's, but still fully indebted to what came before. Straight male movie stars were praised for adapting a fashion that was clearly rooted in queerness.

CHADWICK BOSEMAN'S SILVER SHOULDERS

The late Chadwick Boseman had just become one of the biggest, most important movie stars on the planet when he attended the 2018 Oscars. *Black Panther* had come out the month prior and was well on its way to breaking records. Attending as a presenter—the following year the film would be nominated for Best Picture—Boseman opted for an overcoat with silk lapels and silver embroidery embellishing the shoulders. The look was designed by Givenchy Haute Couture. He wore David Yurman jewelry, and sleek boots with zippers up the front. The outfit seemed designed to recall his superheroic alter ego, and the press responded in kind, anointing him. "Chadwick Boseman was the king of the Oscars red carpet," one headline declared. Another echoed the same sentiment: "Chadwick Boseman's Jacket Is King of the 2018 Oscars Red Carpet." But it wasn't just that he shouted "Wakanda forever" on the red carpet, further establishing his royalty, it was that his coat challenged expectations for what a male movie star, one currently in the biggest action franchise around, should wear to the Oscars.

When Boseman's predecessors attempted long jackets, they were pilloried. Boseman's tailoring was better, yes, but the experimentation was also rewarded because it offered a different, more challenging vision of what an action hero could look like. He could sparkle.

The following year, Boseman got even bolder, once again with help from Givenchy. He wore beads trailing down his back and a scarf. From certain angles it almost looked as if he were wearing a dress instead of pants. And it didn't matter. Rachel Tashjian, writing for *GQ*, hailed Boseman as part of a new wave of men's fashion, one which embraced the artistry of designers. "Men are eager to experiment with our vision of 'formal' on the red carpet, and our definition of masculinity," she wrote.

As an actor, Boseman played legends of history, fictional and otherwise. On the red carpet, he charted a blazing trail.

2021 OSCARS

WHEN CHLOÉ ZHAO BECAME THE SECOND WOMAN EVER in Oscars' history to win Best Director in 2021, she wore sneakers. They were Hermés sneakers, but they were still sneakers, plain white sneakers, clearly visible under her ankle-length dress. (Also Hermés.) And she wasn't the only woman to choose comfort alongside couture while making history that night. Emerald Fennell opted for matching Gucci trainers under her Gucci gown as she claimed Best Original Screenplay, making her the first woman since Diablo Cody to win any sort of writing award. But while Fennell's were almost a secret, hidden under her floral frock, Zhao's were there for everyone to see.

It was hard to imagine how Zhao would dress up for the occasion. The Chinese-born auteur did not seem like the type of person to embrace luxury. Her film, *Nomadland*, was her first made with any sort of professional actors, and it was a roving epic about a widow, played by Frances McDormand, who lives out of her van, poverty forcing her to choose a roaming life-style. Despite being feted with glossy photo shoots throughout the extended Oscar season, Zhao remained true to her own low-key style. She wore her hair either long and flowing or in braids. She chose pants over skirts. When she appeared, via webcam, at the Golden Globes she appeared to just be wear-ing a simple T-shirt.

Of course, nothing about the Oscars in 2021 was normal, just like nothing about 2021 at all was normal. The coronavi-rus pandemic forced most major blockbusters for the awards cycle out of theaters, which largely remained closed through-out 2020 and into 2021. To account for the circumstances, the Academy postponed the awards until late April, also extend-ing the window of eligibility. The venue was changed from the traditional Dolby Theatre to Los Angeles's historic metro hub, Union Station. Oscar producers Steven Soderbergh, Sta-cey Cher, and Jesse Collins opted for an intimate ceremony with guests gathered around tables. But they still encouraged

"Inspirational and Aspirational" fashion. Perhaps sneakers were not what they were thinking, but Zhao and Fennell more than completed the assignment. Neither woman looked like she had just rolled out of bed after a year of quarantine, but they did what so many have been dreaming of doing for ages: giving their feet a rest. And they were celebrated for it. *Vogue*, which has too frequently upheld unreasonable standards throughout its history, wrote: "Chloé Zhao Proves the White Sneaker Is the Perfect Shoe for Any Occasion, Including the Oscars."

Footwear has for years been the source of controversy for women in Hollywood. At the Cannes Film Festival, women are still banned from wearing anything but heels on the red carpet. Going into the night, Zhao likely knew she was going to win, and instead of trying to conform to what a female Oscar winner should look like, she chose to mold it in her own image. After all, she was going to be a trailblazer no matter what: the first woman of color to win Best Director in the awards' 93-year history. Future generations will have to follow in her sneaker-covered steps.

the future of Oscar Fashion

THE ACADEMY AWARDS ARE VERY SLOW TO PROGRESS. They are a tradition defined by stasis and reliability. Wars and global pandemics can only *delay* the Oscars, not cancel them. And thus, the ceremony will inch toward change. The same can be said for style. It's cyclical, yes, but notions of what is "classy"—as restrictive as that term might be—are pretty consistent over the years. That's why certain looks are timeless, like the ones I've described worn by Mary Pickford, Audrey Hepburn, Michelle Williams, and Lupita Nyong'o. But it's also why breaking the trend of what's acceptable is a risk, especially for women.

Predicting what the fashion of the future will be is a rather ridiculous endeavor and can have people envisioning *Back to the Future Part II* or *Zenon: Girl of the 21st Century*. At the Oscars, there will always be women in floor-length gowns in the preferred cut of the day. But as the institution diversifies so will, hopefully, the ideas of what is quote-unquote beautiful. Widening the scope of who and what gets honored by the

Academy will also open the door for more experimentation. And no matter what happens, it will always remain the case that the categories "best" and "worst" dressed are too limiting to encompass what outfits really mean to the people who wear them.

acknowledgments

I'd like to thank the Academy. Just kidding, although I guess it does have some role in this. More importantly, I'd like to thank my editor, Shannon Fabricant, designer Susan Van Horn, and the whole team at Running Press. This is my second book with the imprint, and it's all been a delight. As an editor, Shannon is so wise and supports my vision every step of the way. As a friend, she is a Taylor Swift expert with fabulous style. Montana Forbes is the illustrator of my dreams. Her ability to capture the nuances of fashion is incredible. My genius agent Christopher Hermelin helped turn this from an idea into a coherent and elegant pitch.

Bob Marshall, you're my favorite person and I love you, and thank you for encouraging me to write a book during a pandemic when we moved across the country. My parents, Darlene Kaplan and Steve Zuckerman, instilled in me a love of cinema and the ability to hustle. To my aunt, Cathy Kaplan, I would not have my love of fashion if it weren't for you. Daisy, you're my dog, and I'm obsessed with you. Thanks for the kisses and cuteness.

My Thrillist family: You guys are the best. Lindsay Gellman, you're an amazing friend and an amazing sounding board. Amy Nicholson, I'm so indebted to you for taking a look at this draft. Joe Reid, your treasure trove of Oscar ceremonies was invaluable. Lindsey Weber, thank you for accepting the early version of this pitch as a series for Medium. The team at Bob Mackie—Jenelle Hamilton and Joe McFate— helped me get in touch with a legend. Mr. Mackie, thank you for being so generous with your time. To the writers and historians cited in this book: I could not have done this without you paving the way. I'm so proud of this project. It came true.

notes

p. 2: In 2015, the #AskHerMore campaign: "Reese Witherspoon Slams Sexist Red Carpet Questions," *Time*, https://time.com/3718008/oscars-2015-askhermore-reese-witherspoon/, accessed 14 Feb. 2021.

p. 3: Louis B. Mayer invented the Academy: David Thomson, "The Oscars Were Invented To Break Up Hollywood Unions: The True, Surprising History of the Academy Awards," *Vanity Fair*, https://www.vanityfair.com/hollywood/2014/02/secret-oscar-history, accessed 14 Feb. 2021.

p. 3: His notion was: Jackie Mansky, "The First Academy Awards Had Its Own Version of the 'Popular' Oscar," *Smithsonian Magazine*, https://www.smithsonianmag.com/arts-culture/subtle-union-busting-roots-original-popular-oscar-1-180969955/, accessed 14 Feb. 2021.

p. 4: "Red-carpet commentators enforce a code of conduct": Haley Mlotek, "When Did the Red Carpet Become Prom?" *New York Times*, 26 Feb. 2016, https://www.nytimes.com/2016/02/26/magazine/when-did-the-red-carpet-become-prom.html.

p. 5: April Reign was watching: Reggie Ugwu, "The Hashtag That Changed the Oscars: An Oral History," *New York Times*, 6 Feb. 2020, https://www.nytimes.com/2020/02/06/movies/oscarssowhite-history.html.

p. 5: To combat the long-entrenched: Glenn Whipp. "Gold Standard: What the New, Vastly Expanded Academy Membership Could Mean for the Oscars," *Los Angeles Times*, 26 June 2018, https://www.latimes.com/entertainment/movies/la-et-mn-academy-membership-gold-standard-20180626-story.html.

p. 9: It's strikingly casual: Nadra Nittle, "Why Nobody Knows What Stars Wore to the First Academy Awards," *Racked*, 1 Mar. 2018, https://www.racked.com/2018/3/1/17064712/first-oscars-1929-outfits-academy-awards.

p. 9: The awards were a banquet: Gail Kinn and Jim Piazza, *The Academy Awards: The Complete Unofficial History* (New York: Black Dog & Leventhal, 2014), 11.

p. 9: A committee of five judges: Gail Kinn and Jim Piazza, *The Academy Awards: The Complete Unofficial History* (New York: Black Dog & Leventhal, 2014), 12, 14.

p. 11: Born Gladys Smith in Toronto: "Mary Pickford: America's First Screen Megastar," *Guardian*, 25 Apr. 2016, http://www.theguardian.com/film/2016/apr/25/mary-pickford-silent-film-megastar-gladys-smith-actor-producer-mogul.

p. 11: She started as a teenager: Kristin Hunt, "Mary Pickford Knew Not to Take the First Offer," JSTOR Daily, 7 Nov. 2019, https://daily.jstor.org/mary-pickford-knew-not-to-take-the-first-offer/.

p. 11: Pickford initially believed: Scott Eyman. *Mary Pickford, America's Sweetheart* (D.I. Fine, 1990), 39.

p. 11: She was instrumental: "Mary Pickford and the Academy of Motion Pictures Arts & Sciences," Mary Pickford Foundation, 18 Apr. 2017, https://marypickford.org/caris-articles/mary-pickford-academy/.

p. 11: She was consistently cast as children: "Mary Pickford: America's First Screen Megastar," *Guardian*, 25 Apr. 2016, http://www.theguardian.com/film/2016/apr/25/mary-pickford-silent-film-megastar-gladys-smith-actor-producer-mogul.

p. 12: Her mother, who had served: Scott Eyman, *Mary Pickford, America's Sweetheart* (D.I. Fine, 1990), 185.

p. 12: "They had been my making": "Mary Cuts Her Hair," Mary Pickford Foundation, 20 June 2018, https://marypickford.org/caris-articles/mary-cuts-her-hair/.

p. 13: "Miss Pickford herself chose": Mordaunt Hall, "THE SCREEN (Published 1929)," *New York Times*, 6 Apr. 1929, https://www.nytimes.com/1929/04/06/archives/the-screen.html.

p. 13: She invited the Academy's Board: Damien Bona, "OSCAR FILMS; 75 Years of Bribes, Lies and Overkill (Published 2003)," *New York Times*, 9 Mar. 2003, https://www.nytimes.com/2003/03/09/movies/oscar-films-75-years-of-bribes-lies-and-overkill.html.

p. 13: How did she acquire: Bronwyn Cosgrave, *Made for Each Other: Fashion and the Academy Awards*. (London: Bloomsbury, 2007).

p. 14: Her purchases became a minor scandal: MARY PICKFORD TO PAY $3,900 TO GET TRUNKS; Customs Fixes Duty on $7,268 Value for Clothes but Does Not Impose Fine. http://timesmachine.nytimes.com/timesmachine/1928/06/20/95586842.html?pageNumber=15, accessed 6 Apr. 2021.

p. 14: "Fragonard Blue": Bronwyn Cosgrave, *Made for Each Other: Fashion and the Academy Awards*. (London: Bloomsbury, 2007).

p. 14: One of the persistent myths: Amy Nicholson, "What's Behind The Best Supporting Actress Curse? Plain, Old, Unmagical Sexism," NPR, https://www.npr.org/2016/02/24/467949931/whats-behind-the-best-supporting-actress-curse-plain-old-unmagical-sexism, accessed 22 Nov. 2020.

p. 14: "I left the screen": "Mary Pickford: America's First Screen Megastar," *Guardian*, 25 Apr. 2016, http://www.theguardian.com/film/2016/apr/25/mary-pickford-silent-film-megastar-gladys-smith-actor-producer-mogul.

p. 15: "I desire a white casket": "Black Actress May Get Part of Wish," AP, https://apnews.com/article/05bb7177c94a48fdb5d0693d48e751f7, accessed 14 Dec. 2020.

p. 15: "The reason why": "Mo'Nique Honors Actress Hattie McDaniel at Oscars," ABC7 Chicago, https://abc7chicago.com/archive/7317781/, accessed 14 Dec. 2020.

p. 17: In Rita Dove's poem: "Hattie McDaniel Arrives at the Coconut Grove," Poetry Archive, https://poetryarchive.org/poem/hattie-mcdaniel-arrives-at-coconut-grove/, accessed 14 Dec. 2020.

p. 18: McDaniel was born the daughter: Jill Watts, *Hattie McDaniel: Black Ambition, White Hollywood* (New York: Amistad, 2007), 1, 2.

p. 18: she "bravely attacked": Jill Watts, *Hattie McDaniel: Black Ambition, White Hollywood* (New York: Amistad, 2007), 40.

p. 18: she had read the book three times: Don Ryan, "Yoohoo! Hi'ya Hattie!" *Los Angeles Times Sunday Magazine*, 11 Feb. 1940, 20.

p. 18: By that time, she was known in Hollywood: Jill Watts, *Hattie McDaniel: Black Ambition, White Hollywood* (New York: Amistad, 2007), 139–40.

p. 19: The criticism would continue: Jill Watts, *Hattie McDaniel: Black Ambition, White Hollywood* (New York: Amistad, 2007), 156.

p. 19: "she is being a Mammy in real life": Jill Watts, *Hattie McDaniel: Black Ambition, White Hollywood* (New York: Amistad, 2007), 162.

p. 19: "the brave efficient type of womanhood": Jill Watts, *Hattie McDaniel: Black Ambition, White Hollywood* (New York: Amistad, 2007), 176.

p. 19: The *LA Times Sunday Magazine* profile: Don Ryan, "Yoohoo! Hi'ya Hattie!" *Los Angeles Times Sunday Magazine*, 11 Feb. 1940, 8.

p. 20: "If you had seen her face": Louella Parsons, "Hattie McDaniel Is the First Negro to Get Coveted Motion Picture Award," *Tyler Courier-Times*, 10 Mar. 1940, 6.

p. 21: Under contract first with Selznick: Jill Watts, *Hattie McDaniel: Black Ambition, White Hollywood* (New York: Amistad, 2007), 205.

p. 21: Her Oscar, the plaque: W. Burlette Carter, "Finding the Oscar," SSRN Scholarly Paper, ID 1980721, Social Science Research Network, 6 Jan. 2012, https://papers.ssrn.com/abstract=1980721.

p. 22: After her victory she, too: "Mo'nique Went from Oscar Winner to Hollywood Pariah. Can She Bounce Back?" *Washington Post*, https://www.washingtonpost.com/news/style/wp/2019/02/07/feature/monique-went-from-oscar-winner-to-hollywood-pariah-can-she-bounce-back/, accessed 19 Dec. 2020.

p. 24: Davis had a plan: "Flashback: When Bette Davis Became the Academy's First Female President — and Resigned in Disgust," *Hollywood Reporter*, https://www.hollywoodreporter.com/race/flashback-bette-davis-became-academys-868014, accessed 28 Dec. 2020.

p. 24: The official line was "ill health": Louella O. Parsons, "Dispute Caused Bette Davis To Quite Academy Presidency," *San Francisco Examiner*, 29 Dec. 1941, 24.

p. 24: The Board of Governors eventually: "Will Hold Academy Dinner After All, But Nix Finery, Hoofing and Glitter," *Variety*, 4 Feb. 1942.

p. 24: According to the official Academy memo: Bronwyn Cosgrave, *Made for Each Other: Fashion and the Academy Awards* (London: Bloomsbury, 2007).

p. 25: After the war there was a return: "How To Dress for the Oscars," Oscars. Org | Academy of Motion Picture Arts and Sciences, 11 Feb. 2015, https://www.oscars.org/news/how-dress-oscars.

p. 25: "really a referee": "Famed Designer Edith Head Consultant," *Valley Times*, 19 Apr. 1966, 36.

p. 26: "hideous miniskirt": Dorothy Manners, "Afterthoughts on Oscar," *San Francisco Examiner*, 14 April 1967.

p. 26: The frenzy over the little dress: Sidney Skolsky, "Fade Out, In for Hollywood," *Citizen-News*, 13 May 1967, 14.

p. 27: In a letter sent to nominees: "Oscars: Producers Detail 'Safe,' 'Intimate' Ceremony in Letter to Nominees." *The Hollywood Reporter*, 18 Mar. 2021, https://www.hollywoodreporter.com/race/oscars-producers-detail-safe-intimate-ceremony-in-letter-to-nominees.

p. 30: "fluffy blue nightgown": UP, "Joan Crawford collects first 'Oscar' after 21 years of trying," *Lincoln Journal Star*, 8 Mar. 1946, 5.

p. 30: It was designed by Helen Rose: Patty Fox, *Star Style at the Academy Awards: A Century of Glamour* (Santa Monica, CA: Angel City Press, 2000), 45.

p. 30: "Flu coupled with the nervous tension": Joan Crawford, *A Portrait of Joan: The Autobiography of Joan Crawford* (Papamoa Press, 2017).

p. 30: Still, the gossip goes: Julie Miller, "The Academy Award That Joan Crawford Accepted in Bed Sells; Can You Guess for How Much?" *Vanity Fair*, https://www.vanityfair.com/hollywood/2012/09/joan-crawford-academy-award-auction, accessed 18 Jan. 2021.

p. 31: "I voted for Bergman myself": UP, "Joan Crawford collects first 'Oscar' after 21 years of trying," *Lincoln Journal Star*, 8 Mar. 1946, 5.

p. 31: she had been trying: UP, "Joan Crawford collects first 'Oscar' after 21 years of trying," *Lincoln Journal Star*, 8 Mar. 1946, 5.

p. 31: "I sailed into Mildred": Joan Crawford, *A Portrait of Joan: The Autobiography of Joan Crawford* (Papamoa Press, 2017).

p. 32: Just a week later: AP, "Joan Crawford Seeks Divorce," *San Bernadino County Sun*, 12 Mar. 1946, 1.

p. 33: She wasn't predicted to win: Barry Paris, *Audrey Hepburn* (New York: Berkley, 2001).

p. 35: "has been described as 'romantic; fey; puckish'": Elsie Lee, "Audrey's Search for Love," *Screenland*, Nov. 1953, 36.

p. 36: It's widely considered: "See Audrey Hepburn's Most Iconic Givenchy Looks," *The Cut*, 3 Apr. 2016, https://www.thecut.com/2016/04/audrey-hepburn-givenchy-fashion-love-affair.html.

p. 36: "It is definitely not by Givenchy": Esther Zuckerman, "How Audrey Hepburn Cultivated Influence Through a Simple Neckline," *Medium*, 1 Mar. 2018, https://medium.com/s/who-are-you-wearing/how-audrey-hepburn-cultivated-her-influence-through-a-simple-neckline-c696838f5f3a.

p. 36: Hepburn, daughter of a Dutch baroness: "'Those Are Things You Don't Forget.' How a Young Audrey Hepburn Helped the Dutch Resistance During World War II," *Time*, https://time.com/5582729/audrey-hepburn-world-war-ii/, accessed 29 Dec. 2020.

p. 37: In the lead-up to Oscar night: Amy Fine Collins, "The Style Marriage of Givenchy and Audrey Hepburn," *Vanity Fair*, https://www.vanityfair.com/style/2014/02/audrey-hepburn-givenchy-style, accessed 29 Dec. 2020.

p. 37: Audrey "went above Head": Bronwyn Cosgrave, *Made for Each Other: Fashion and the Academy Awards* (London: Bloomsbury, 2007).

p. 38: "I told Audrey": Amy Fine Collins, "The Style Marriage of Givenchy and Audrey Hepburn," *Vanity Fair*, https://www.vanityfair.com/style/2014/02/audrey-hepburn-givenchy-style, accessed 29 Dec. 2020.

p. 38: Head maintained that she was responsible: "Edith Head and the 'Sabrina' Dress," *Los Angeles Times*, 24 Oct. 2010, https://www.latimes.com/archives/la-xpm-2010-oct-24-la-ig-edithredux-20101024-story.html.

p. 39: When Emma Stone accepted: Erika Harwood, "Emma Stone's Unexpected Oscar Connection to Audrey Hepburn," *Vanity Fair*, https://www.vanityfair.com/style/2017/02/emma-stone-audrey-hepburn-givenchy-oscars, accessed 29 Dec. 2020.

p. 40: "What a cute thing she was": Louella Parsons, "After-Thoughts on the Academy Awards," *Modern Screen*, Feb.-Dec. 1958, 18.

p. 42: She retired from acting: "Why Did Miyoshi Umeki, the Only Asian Actress to Ever Win an Oscar, Destroy Her Trophy?" *Entertainment Weekly*, https://ew.com/oscars/2018/02/22/miyoshi-umeki-sayonara-oscars-profile/, accessed 10 Jan. 2021.

p. 42: she threw away her Oscar: "Why Did Miyoshi Umeki, the Only Asian Actress to Ever Win an Oscar, Destroy Her Trophy?" *Entertainment Weekly*, https://ew.com/oscars/2018/02/22/miyoshi-umeki-sayonara-oscars-profile/, accessed 10 Jan. 2021.

p. 44: Umeki was born in Hokkaido: AP, "American Success Story Told by Miyoshi Umeki, Oscar Winner." *The Post-Crescent*, 28 Mar. 1958, 18.

p. 44: she was performing at a club: AP, "American Success Story Told by Miyoshi Umeki, Oscar Winner." *The Post-Crescent*, 28 Mar. 1958, 18.

p. 44: She appeared on a variety show: "Obituary: Miyoshi Umeki," *Guardian*, 17 Sept. 2007, http://www.theguardian.com/news/2007/sep/17/guardianobituaries.japan.

p. 45: The *Post-Crescent* from Appleton: AP, "American Success Story Told by Miyoshi Umeki, Oscar Winner," *Post Crescent*, 28 Mar. 1958, 18.

p. 45: The *Marshfield News-Herald*, also from Wisconsin: Patrick McNulty, "Jap Winner of Oscar Is Elated," *Marshfield News-Herald*, 28 Mar. 1958, 2.

p. 45: "How can you lose": Louella Parsons, "Last of four articles on new feminine stars in Hollywood," *Philadelphia Inquirer*, 5 Nov. 1958, 37.

p. 46: If Woodward hadn't said: AP, "Joanne Woodward, Alec Guinness Winners of Hollywood Oscars," *Asbury Park Press*, 27 Mar. 1958, 2.

p. 46: "I didn't think I had a chance": AP, "Joanne Woodward, Alec Guinness Winners of Hollywood Oscars," *Asbury Park Press*, 27 Mar. 1958, 2.

p. 47: Woodward was still a fairly new face: Linn Unkefer, "The Joanne Woodward Story: Corned Beef Hash to Oscar in a Year," *Detroit Free-Press*, 28 Mar. 1958, 42.

p. 48: he "kept insisting": Sam Berns, "Hollywood," *Motion Picture Daily*, 31 Mar. 1958.

p. 48: a profile of Woodward highlighting: Linn Unkefer, "The Joanne Woodward Story: Corned Beef Hash to Oscar in a Year," *Detroit Free-Press*, 28 Mar. 1958, 42.

p. 48: "I spent nearly $100 for the material": "See What's New?" *Pomona Progress Bulletin*, 9 June 1958, 19.

p. 48: "I thought I would wear it again": Erskine Johnson, "New Disney Film Stars 'Talking' Shaggy Dog," *Lancaster New Era*, 5 Aug. 1958, 15.

p. 49: Woodward went to college: Kathleen Teltsch, "Newman To Endow New Chair (Published 1991)," *New York Times*, 27 Mar. 1991, https://www.nytimes.com/1991/03/27/news/newman-to-endow-new-chair.html.

p. 49: "encouraging undergraduates": Kathleen Teltsch, "Newman To Endow New Chair (Published 1991)," *New York Times*, 27 Mar. 1991, https://www.nytimes.com/1991/03/27/news/newman-to-endow-new-chair.html.

p. 51: "Rita Moreno is honestly an inspiration": Emma Dibdin, "Rita Moreno Re-Wore Her Oscar Gown From The 1962 Oscars At The 2018 Oscars," *Cosmopolitan*, 5 Mar. 2018, https://www.cosmopolitan.com/entertainment/movies/a19078199/oscars-2018-rita-moreno-recycled-gown-1962/.

p. 51: "recycling has never been more elegant": Maya Salam, "Rita Moreno in Her 1962 Oscars Gown in 2018 (Published 2018)," *New York Times*, 5 Mar. 2018, https://www.nytimes.com/2018/03/04/style/rita-moreno-1962-oscars-dress.html.

p. 52: Moreno—as she told Ryan Seacrest: "Rita Moreno Wears Her 1962 Oscar Win Dress to 2018 Oscars," E! Red Carpet & Award Shows—YouTube, https://www.youtube.com/watch?v=rz7gkilcxUA, accessed 24 Dec. 2020.

p. 52: "I ordered a heavily brocaded dress": Rita Moreno, *Rita Moreno: A Memoir* (New York: Penguin Group, 2013), 130.

p. 53: "Why oh why do Latin girls": Bob Thomas, "Latin's Aren't Spitfires," Associated Press, 18 Nov. 1960.

p. 53: "the studio brass": John D. Weaver, "Hollywood's Most Outspoken Actress," *Holiday Magazine*, Nov. 1961, 119.

p. 53: "At this point": Rita Moreno, *Rita Moreno: A Memoir* (New York: Penguin Group, 2013), 183.

p. 53: She was frustrated: Rita Morena, *Rita Moreno: A Memoir* (New York: Penguin Group, 2013), 187.

p. 54: "least favorable cliché": The New York Times: Best Pictures, https://archive.nytimes.com/www.nytimes.com/packages/html/movies/bestpictures/west-re.html, accessed 24 Dec. 2020.

p. 54: "Afterward, I had a hollow feeling": Rita Moreno, *Rita Moreno: A Memoir* (New York: Penguin Group, 2013), 173.

p. 54: It was a "paycheck": Rita Moreno, *Rita Moreno: A Memoir* (New York: Penguin Group, 2013), 173

p. 55: her friend told her how her victory: Rita Moreno, *Rita Moreno: A Memoir* (New York: Penguin Group, 2013), 191–92.

p. 55: "My career was certainly on the wane": Jack Smith, "Rita Moreno, Cheered by Oscar, Buys a Hat," *Los Angeles Times*, 11 Apr. 1962, 37.

p. 55: "The power of the Academy Award": Leonard Harris, "Oscar No Aid to Rita Moreno," *New York World-Telegram*, 5 Oct. 1964, 10.

p. 56: To this day, Moreno is one of only four: Clayton Davis, "Why Are Latino Actors Still the Oscars' Weak Spot?" *Variety*, 29 Sept. 2020, https://variety.com/2020/film/awards/oscars-latino-actors-1234785622/.

p. 56: the same year that Moreno revived: Laura Bradley, "Oscars 2018 Was a Celebration of Latinx Talent—With No Latinx Acting Nominees," *Vanity Fair*, https://www.vanityfair.com/hollywood/2018/03/oscars-2018-latinx-representation-guillermo-del-toro-best-director-best-picture, accessed 24 Dec. 2020.

p. 56: "One interesting observation": Clayton Davis, "Why Are Latino Actors Still the Oscars' Weak Spot?" *Variety*, 29 Sept. 2020, https://variety.com/2020/film/awards/oscars-latino-actors-1234785622/.

p. 59: "I wanted a white collar and cuffs": "The Eternal Star Power of Barbra Streisand," *W Magazine* | Women's Fashion & Celebrity News, https://www.wmagazine.com/story/barbra-streisand-interview-w-magazine-photographed-steven-meisel/, accessed 12 Dec. 2020.

p. 60: "When, five years ago, 16-year-old Barbra": Shana Alexander, "A born loser's success and precarious love," *Life*, 22 May 1964.

p. 60: "carelessly stacked girl": "The Girl," *Time*, 10 Apr. 1964, 62–67.

p. 61: She was also, somewhat controversially: "When Gregory Peck Defended Barbra Streisand's Oscars Membership," *Hollywood Reporter*, https://www.hollywoodreporter.com/news/gregory-peck-defended-barbra-streisands-oscars-membership-1191304, accessed 11 Dec. 2020.

p. 61: "When she is singing": *The Screen: Launching Pad for Barbra Strei-sand*, https://archive.nytimes.com/www.nytimes.com/books/97/04/27/reviews/streisand-bow.html, accessed 11 Dec. 2020.

p. 61: "Let's show people how young and cute": Eugenia Sheppard, "Why Bar-bra Forgot that 'Elegant Bit,'" *Los Angeles Times*, 21 Apr. 1969, 79.

p. 62: "lovely, but very conservative": "The Eternal Star Power of Barbra Strei-sand," *W Magazine* | Women's Fashion & Celebrity News, https://www.wmagazine.com/story/barbra-streisand-interview-w-magazine-photo-graphed-steven-meisel/, accessed 12 Dec. 2020.

p. 62: "see-through thing was yeuch": Belle Greenberg, "From Where I Sit," *Hollywood Citizen News*, 18 Apr. 1969, 33.

p. 62: Streisand had to remove her gum: Kirsten Chuba, "Barbra Streisand Recalls Winning the Best Actress Oscar for 'Funny Girl,'" *Variety*, 1 Mar. 2018, https://variety.com/video/barbra-streisand-funny-girl-oscar/.

p. 64: Lawrence, having just crowed: "Watch Jennifer Lawrence Crave McDon-ald's at the Oscars," *Grub Street*, https://www.grubstreet.com/2013/02/jennifer-lawrence-mcdonalds.html, accessed 12 Dec. 2020.

p. 65: By the time the awards season: "Jennifer Lawrence Lands Dior Campaign." The Cut, https://www.thecut.com/2012/10/jennifer-law-rence-lands-dior-campaign.html, accessed 10 Apr. 2021.

p. 65: "That's the problem with the Oscars": "This Week in Jennifer Lawrence Quotes: Sweatpants, Carpools, and Step Brothers," *Vulture*, https://www.vulture.com/2013/02/this-week-in-jennifer-lawrence-quotes.html, accessed 13 Dec. 2020.

p. 66: "I was at the Oscars, waiting to hear": "Best Performances: See Hol-lywood's Biggest Stars," *W Magazine* | Women's Fashion & Celebrity News, https://www.wmagazine.com/gallery/best-performances-holly-wood-juergen-teller/, accessed 13 Dec. 2020.

p. 66: The fall was immediately branded: Esther Zuckerman, "Jennifer Law-rence Tripping Is a Moment That Will Live in Oscar Infamy," *Atlantic*, 25 Feb. 2013, https://www.theatlantic.com/culture/archive/2013/02/jenni-fer-lawrence-tripping-oscars/318018/.

p. 67: "That night felt different": Jane Fonda, *My Life: So Far* (New York: Ran-dom House, 2005), 319.

p. 69: Her mug shot became a sensation: Mackenzie Wagoner, "Jane Fonda's 1970 Mug Shot Started a Beauty Revolution 47 Years Ago Today," *Vogue*, https://www.vogue.com/article/jane-fonda-hair-mugshot-1970-klute-an-niversary-vietnam-war, accessed 26 Dec. 2020.

p. 69: "I wore something that made a statement": Bronwyn Cosgrave, "Jane Fonda: The Reluctant Fashionista (Published 2016)," *New York Times*, 21 Sept. 2016, https://www.nytimes.com/2016/09/22/fashion/jane-fon-da-clothing-auction.html.

p. 69: Fonda, as she frequently said at the time: Mary Blume, "Jane Fonda an Optimist of the Soul," *Los Angeles Times*, 20 Feb. 1972, 474.

p. 70: "first public act against the war": Jane Fonda, *My Life: So Far* (New York: Random House, 2005), 317.

p. 70: "My wardrobe was pared down": Jane Fonda, *My Life: So Far* (New York: Random House, 2005), 314.

p. 70: She didn't think she was right: Jane Fonda, *My Life: So Far* (New York: Random House, 2005), 333.

p. 70: "What is it about Jane Fonda": Roger Ebert, "Klute Movie Review & Film Summary (1971) | Roger Ebert," https://www.rogerebert.com/reviews/klute-1971, accessed 26 Dec. 2020.

p. 71: "there isn't another young dramatic actress": Pauline Kael, "The Current Cinema," *New Yorker*, 3 July 1971, 42.

p. 71: "Being hated": Jane Fonda, *My Life: So Far* (New York: Random House, 2005), 339.

p. 71: She arrived on set one day to find an American flag: Jane Fonda, *My Life: So Far* (New York: Random House, 2005), 340.

p. 71: She and *Klute* costar Sutherland: Roger Greenspun, "Jane Fonda's 'F.T.A.' Show Now a Film (Published 1972)," *New York Times*, 22 July 1972, https://www.nytimes.com/1972/07/22/archives/jane-fondas-fta-show-now-a-film.html.

p. 71: "not vindictive": "Scott, Jane Fonda Selections Prove Academy Not Vindictive," UPI, 6 Mar. 1972.

p. 72: That's the kind of minefield: UPI, "Scott, Jane Fonda Selections Prove Academy Not Vindictive," *Progress-Bulletin*, 6 Mar. 1972, 10.

p. 72: The elegant but stark suit: Bronwyn Cosgrave, "Jane Fonda: The Reluctant Fashionista (Published 2016)," *New York Times*, 21 Sept. 2016, https://www.nytimes.com/2016/09/22/fashion/jane-fonda-clothing-auction.html.

p. 72: "Tell 'em there's a lot to say": Jane Fonda, *My Life: So Far* (New York: Random House, 2005), 369.

p. 72: there were some boos: Joyce Haber, "What Oscar Show Needed: Bob Hope," *Los Angeles Times*, 12 Apr. 1972, 89.

p. 72: Decades later, Fonda's choice of dress: Brooke Bobb, "What Jane Fonda's 1972 Oscars Suit Can Teach Us About #MeToo at the Golden Globes," *Vogue*, https://www.vogue.com/article/fashion-runway-golden-globe-awards-2017-metoo-black-dress-code, accessed 26 Dec. 2020.

p. 76: Even Berry Gordy: J. Randy Taraborrelli, *Diana Ross: A Biography* (New York: Citadel, 2007), 301.

p. 76: Gordy told producer Jay Weston: J. Randy Taraborrelli, *Diana Ross: A Biography* (New York: Citadel, 2007), 301.

p. 77: My God what had I done: J. Randy Taraborrelli, *Diana Ross: A Biography* (New York: Citadel, 2007), 311.

p. 77: She was more interested in absorbing: Loraine Alterman, "Pop," *New York Times*, 7 Jan. 1973, https://www.nytimes.com/1973/01/07/archives/you-cant-beat-an-original-pop.html.

p. 77: "one of the great performances of 1972": Roger Ebert, "Lady Sings the Blues Movie Review (1972) | Roger Ebert," https://www.rogerebert.com/reviews/lady-sings-the-blues-1972, accessed 9 Feb. 2021.

p. 77: "living proof that stars who really shine": Michael Thomas, "Diana Ross Goes From Riches to Rags," *Rolling Stone*, 1 Feb. 1973, https://www.rollingstone.com/music/music-news/diana-ross-goes-from-riches-to-rags-165274/.

p. 78: His run of "for your consideration" ads: Pete Hammond, "OSCAR: Melissa Leo Goes Rogue With Her Own Personal Campaign Ads," *Deadline*, 5 Feb. 2011, https://deadline.com/2011/02/oscar-melissa-leo-goes-rogue-with-her-own-personal-campaign-ads-103757/.

p. 78: Gordy even gave Ross a dog: J. Randy Taraborrelli, *Diana Ross: A Biography* (New York: Citadel, 2007), 332.

p. 78: Mackie, best known: Brittany Spanos, "Bob Mackie: My Life in 12 Dresses," *Rolling Stone*, 29 May 2019, https://www.rollingstone.com/culture/culture-features/cher-bob-mackie-dresses-broadway-841553/.

p. 79: Was racism at the root: "A Guide to the Desperate Female Oscar Campaign," https://www.vice.com/en/article/ppmnqy/a-guide-to-the-desperate-female-oscar-campaign-769, accessed 12 Feb. 2021.

p. 80: She called on her stylist: Cicely Tyson, *Just as I Am: A Memoir* (New York: HarperCollins Publishers, 2021), 232.

p. 81: She told the Hollywood reporter: "Cicely Tyson Reflects on Her Iconic Fashion Moments: 'You Can Bet Your Bottom Dollar It Stops the Show,'" *Hollywood Reporter*, 18 Jan. 2021, https://www.hollywoodreporter.com/lifestyle/style/cicely-tyson-reflects-on-her-iconic-fashion-moments-you-can-bet-your-bottom-dollar-it-stops-the-show-4114886/.

p. 81: "complete with a heart cut-out": Cicely Tyson, *Just as I Am: A Memoir* (New York: HarperCollins Publishers, 2021), 234.

p. 81: "The Black woman has always been shown": Louise Sweeney, "Sounding Out Cicely Tyson," *Democrat and Chronicle*, 21 Jan. 1973, 110.

p. 82: Tyson describes how unsurprised: Cicely Tyson, *Just as I Am: A Memoir* (New York: HarperCollins Publishers, 2021), 234.

p. 82: tried to impede: Cicely Tyson, *Just as I Am: A Memoir* (New York: HarperCollins Publishers, 2021), 232.

p. 82: "I wanted no part": Cicely Tyson, *Just as I Am: A Memoir* (New York: HarperCollins Publishers, 2021), 232.

p. 84: A juvenile award was handed out: "Why the Academy Should Bring Back the Juvenile Oscar," *Hollywood Reporter*, https://www.hollywoodreporter.com/race/why-academy-should-bring-back-juvenile-oscar-968305, accessed 20 Dec. 2020.

p. 85: "It was something of a surprise": Addison Verrill. "Bit-By-Bit (Or Yawn-By-Yawn) Rundown of Oscar Awards Night," *Variety*, 10 Apr. 1974, 6.

p. 86: "strange little girl": Tatum O'Neal, *A Paper Life* (New York: Harper, 2005), 40.

p. 86: "This was the first opportunity": Bruce Fretts, "Oscars Rewind: A Charming Win Filled With Drama and Rancor (Published 2019)," *New York Times*, 18 Jan. 2019, https://www.nytimes.com/2019/01/18/movies/tatum-oneal-oscars.html.

p. 86: He punched her: Tatum O'Neal, *A Paper Life* (New York: Harper, 2005), 63.

p. 86: "I was a big fan of fashion": "Tatum O'Neal Remembers Her 1974 Oscar Win, Shares Advice for Jennifer Lawrence (Q&A)," *Hollywood Reporter*, 27 Feb. 2014, https://www.hollywoodreporter.com/news/oscars-tatum-oneal-remembers-her-682971.

p. 87: "There was no fanfare": Tatum O'Neal, *A Paper Life* (New York: Harper, 2005), 65.

p. 88: "first and only" interview: "A Young Star Is Born in 'Piano' : Movies: Novice Anna Paquin, 11, Who Has Received a Golden Globe Nomination for Best Supporting Actress, Retraces the Fairy-Tale Road She Has Traveled," *Los Angeles Times*, 11 Jan. 1994, https://www.latimes.com/archives/la-xpm-1994-01-11-ca-10819-story.html.

p. 89: "charmed the cynical pressroom": Danielle Morton, "Winners turn serious in Oscar's afterglow," *Pasadena Star News*, 22 Mar. 1994, 7.

p. 89: "tacky": Helen A.S. Popkin, "Child Star," *Tampa Bay-Times*, 28 Mar. 1994, 36.

p. 89: "My Oscar?": Rosanna Greenstreet, "Anna Paquin: 'My Oscar? It's Not the Highlight of My Career,'" *Guardian*, 27 July 2019, https://www.theguardian.com/lifeandstyle/2019/jul/27/anna-paquin-interview-oscar-not-highlight-of-career.

p. 90: She told Ellen DeGeneres: "Quvenzhané Wallis Youngest Oscar Nominee: Puppy Purse," *People*, https://people.com/style/the-must-have-accessory-at-the-oscars-a-puppy-purse/, accessed 21 Dec. 2020.

p. 91: "Everyone else seems afraid": "Oscars: The Onion Under Fire for Calling Quvenzhane Wallis the C-Word," *Hollywood Reporter*, https://www.hollywoodreporter.com/news/onion-calls-quvenzhane-wallis-c-424113, accessed 21 Dec. 2020.

p. 91: The *Onion* apologized: "The Onion and Quvenzhane Wallis: Why Apologize?" *Entertainment Weekly*, https://ew.com/article/2013/02/25/the-onion-apologizes-quvenzhane-wallis/, accessed 21 Dec. 2020.

p. 95: In 1981, Ebert himself: Roger Ebert and Field News Service, "The Last Starlet," *Washington Post*, 27 May 1981, https://www.washingtonpost.com/archive/lifestyle/1981/05/27/the-last-starlet/cf98ac36-8f30-421a-b32e-525f5c9f8935/.

p. 96: "I have a good sense of humor": Edy Williams on Hot Seat with Wally George, www.youtube.com, https://www.youtube.com/watch?v=AUXo-83jAKIw, accessed 11 Apr. 2021.

p. 96: "In response to the controversy": "EDY THE ETERNAL," *Los Angeles Times*, 13 Apr. 1986, https://www.latimes.com/archives/la-xpm-1986-04-13-ca-4277-story.html.

p. 97: "Granted, she doesn't wear very much": "OH, OSCAR," *Los Angeles Times*, 30 Mar. 1986, https://www.latimes.com/archives/la-xpm-1986-03-30-ca-1573-story.html.

p. 98: The showgirl-inspired outfit: Michael Schulman, "A Lifetime of Dressing Cher," *New Yorker*, https://www.newyorker.com/culture/culture-desk/a-lifetime-of-dressing-cher, accessed 31 Dec. 2020.

p. 101: "I wasn't going to go at all": Bruce Weber, "CHER'S NEXT ACT (Published 1987)," *New York Times*, 18 Oct. 1987, https://www.nytimes.com/1987/10/18/magazine/cher-s-next-act.html.

p. 102: "I continue to do really stupid things": "Interview: Cher," *Film Comment*, https://www.filmcomment.com/article/interview-cher/, accessed 2 Jan. 2021.

p. 102: "There's only one fashion question": "Fashion 88 : Mackie & Cher Together Again for the Oscars," *Los Angeles Times*, 8 Apr. 1988, https://www.latimes.com/archives/la-xpm-1988-04-08-vw-1107-story.html.

p. 103: "far from modest": "Cher Wins First Oscar for 'Moonstruck,'" AP, https://apnews.com/article/0a055607635cded09f921c49962971aa, accessed 2 Jan. 2021.

p. 103: She lost an earring: "Jewels of the Oscar," *Los Angeles Times*, 22 Apr. 1988.

p. 104: "I think for a long time": "YEAR IN REVIEW 1995 : Following Her Instincts : In '95 Sharon Stone Finally Hit the Jackpot, with 'Casino.' But Don't Think She's Ready to Cash in Her Chips Just Yet," *Los Angeles Times*, 31 Dec. 1995, https://www.latimes.com/archives/la-xpm-1995-12-31-ca-19470-story.html.

p. 106: "We were making this other great dress": "Sharon Stone Remembers 'Freaking Out' When a FedEx Driver Ran Over Her 1996 Oscars Dress," *People*, https://people.com/style/sharon-stone-says-fedex-driver-ran-over-her-1996-oscars-dress/, accessed 24 Dec. 2020.

p. 107: "Johnny Cash impulse": Sharon Stone, *The Beauty of Living Twice* (Alfred A. Knopf, 2020), 199.

p. 107: It noted that it cost only $22: "Stone tops in Oscar fashion for $22," AP, 29 Mar. 1996.

p. 107: "I felt more grounded": Sharon Stone, *The Beauty of Living Twice* (Alfred A. Knopf, 2020), 199.

p. 107: The ads featured the like of Spike Lee: "How Gap Ruled the '90s," *Grailed*, https://www.grailed.com/drycleanonly/gap-in-the-90s, accessed 24 Dec. 2020.

p. 108: "If there is any doubt": Jennifer Steinhauer and Constance C. R. White, "Women's New Relationship With Fashion (Published 1996)," *New York Times*, 5 Aug. 1996, https://www.nytimes.com/1996/08/05/business/women-s-new-relationship-with-fashion.html.

p. 108: "Never mind her tough-gal reputation": Lloyd Grove, "Sharon's Back in Town | Vanity Fair | March 1996." *Vanity Fair* | The Complete Archive, https://archive.vanityfair.com/article/1996/3/sharons-back-in-town, accessed 24 Dec. 2020.

p. 109: As Bob Dole ran for president: "In Washington, Sharon Stone Meets the Press and Becomes Part of the Show," *Baltimore Sun*, https://webcache.googleusercontent.com/search?q=cache:uBaCnIWo4ncJ:https://www.baltimoresun.com/bs-xpm-1995-06-17-1995168010-story.html+&cd=1&hl=en&ct=clnk&gl=us, accessed 24 Dec. 2020.

p. 109: "In some ways it's male and female fantasies": Bernard Weinraub, "Play a Hooker and Win an Oscar (Published 1996)," *New York Times*, 20 Feb. 1996, https://www.nytimes.com/1996/02/20/movies/play-a-hooker-and-win-an-oscar.html.

p. 112: "I just wanted to look sweet": "The Most Breathtaking Oscars Gowns," *InStyle*, https://www.instyle.com/awards-events/red-carpet/oscars/most-breathtaking-oscars-gowns, accessed 26 Dec. 2020.

p. 112: The movie, a frothy confection: Rebecca Keegan, "Shakespeare in Love and Harvey Weinstein's Dark Oscar Victory," *Vanity Fair*, https://www.vanityfair.com/hollywood/2017/12/shakespeare-in-love-and-harvey-weinsteins-dark-oscar-victory, accessed 27 Dec. 2020.

p. 112: designers were clamoring: Bronwyn Cosgrave, *Made for Each Other: Fashion and the Academy Awards* (London: Bloomsbury, 2007).

p. 112: "very me": "Gwyneth Paltrow Breaks Down 13 Looks From 1995 to Now | Life in Looks | Vogue," YouTube, https://www.youtube.com/watch?v=b-SMbR-V7KqI, accessed 1 May 2021.

p. 113: "Fantastic!" "Perfect!": "The 1999 Oscars: The Fashion," *Entertainment Weekly*, https://ew.com/article/1999/04/02/1999-oscars-fashion/, accessed 27 Dec. 2020.

p. 114: "For the entire evening": "And the Frumps Are ...," *Salon*, 23 Mar. 1999, https://www.salon.com/1999/03/22/cov_22featurea_html/.

p. 114: "Finally, a dress more famous": Emily Gest and Mitchell Fink, "FIANCE: LOVE'S HEALING HINCKLEY?" *New York Daily News*, https://www.nydailynews.com/archives/gossip/fiance-love-healing-hinckley-article-1.829964, accessed 27 Dec. 2020.

p. 114: "didn't fit her very well": "Blythe Danner Hated Gwyneth Paltrow's Pink Oscar Dress," *Us Weekly*, 26 Feb. 2012, https://www.usmagazine.com/stylish/news/blythe-danner-hated-gwyneth-paltrows-pink-oscar-dress-2012262/.

p. 114: she too had been sexually harassed: Jodi Kantor and Rachel Abrams, "Gwyneth Paltrow, Angelina Jolie and Others Say Weinstein Harassed Them (Published 2017)," *New York Times*, 10 Oct. 2017, https://www.nytimes.com/2017/10/10/us/gwyneth-paltrow-angelina-jolie-harvey-weinstein.html.

p. 114: "We were so, like, punk rock": "Holy Shit, 'South Park' Is 20! Trey Parker, Matt Stone on Censors, Tom Cruise and Scientology's Role in Isaac Hayes Quitting," *Hollywood Reporter*, https://www.hollywoodreporter.com/features/south-park-20-years-history-trey-parker-matt-stone-928212, accessed 27 Dec. 2020.

p. 115: It was the fabric responsible: Rachel Tashjian. "How Jennifer Lopez's Versace Dress Created Google Images." *GQ*, https://www.gq.com/story/jennifer-lopez-versace-google-images, accessed 11 Apr. 2021.

p. 115: "Will you change for the parties": "Parker and Stone at Oscars," YouTube, https://www.youtube.com/watch?v=2NlV2gDg48w, accessed 27 Dec. 2020.

p. 115: "super-pissed": "Holy Shit, 'South Park' Is 20! Trey Parker, Matt Stone on Censors, Tom Cruise and Scientology's Role in Isaac Hayes Quitting," *Hollywood Reporter*, https://www.hollywoodreporter.com/features/south-park-20-years-history-trey-parker-matt-stone-928212, accessed 27 Dec. 2020.

p. 116: "It takes a lot of energy": "Holy Shit, 'South Park' Is 20! Trey Parker, Matt Stone on Censors, Tom Cruise and Scientology's Role in Isaac Hayes Quitting," *Hollywood Reporter*, https://www.hollywoodreporter.com/features/south-park-20-years-history-trey-parker-matt-stone-928212, accessed 27 Dec. 2020.

p. 117: starting when she was a child: "GUESS WHO?" *HuffPost*, 15 Feb. 2013, https://www.huffpost.com/entry/angelina-jolie-oscars_n_2694481.

p. 119: That leg became an immediate meme: Hayley Tsukayama, "Angelina Jolie's Leg Finds Its Way onto Statue of Liberty," *Washington Post*, 28 Feb. 2012, https://www.washingtonpost.com/business/technology/angelina-jolies-leg-finds-its-way-onto-statue-of-liberty/2012/02/28/gIQAUpKxfR_story.html.

p. 119: She married Jonny Lee Miller: Alexandra Bandon, "Following, Ambivalently, in Mom or Dad's Footsteps (Published 1996)," *New York Times*, 25 Aug. 1996, https://www.nytimes.com/1996/08/25/movies/following-ambivalently-in-mom-or-dad-s-footsteps.html.

p. 119: A 1999 *Rolling Stone* profile: Mim Udovitch, "The Devil in Miss Angelina Jolie," *Rolling Stone*, 19 Aug. 1999, https://www.rollingstone.com/movies/movie-features/the-devil-in-miss-angelina-jolie-176199/.

p. 120: "weird but memorable": Karen Heller, "They came by twos...," *Sacramento Bee*, 27 Mar. 2000, 51.

p. 120: "fashion victim": Cynthia Robins, "Oscar finery was an elegant eyeful," *San Francisco Examiner*, 27 Mar. 2000, 64.

p. 121: "Angelina had a reputation": "Angelina Jolie's Infamous 2000 Oscars Kiss: An Oral History," *Bustle*, https://www.bustle.com/p/angelina-jo-lies-infamous-2000-oscars-kiss-oral-history-21779886, accessed 23 Jan. 2021.

p. 121: A year after her Oscar win: "Angelina Jolie Named UNHCR Goodwill Ambassador for Refugees," UNHCR, https://www.unhcr.org/news/press/2001/8/3b85044b10/angelina-jolie-named-unhcr-goodwill-am-bassador-refugees.html, accessed 23 Jan. 2021.

p. 122: She later explained: Jessica Bennett, "Why Angelina Jolie Wore Her Iconic Leg-Baring 2012 Oscars Dress," *Page Six*, 1 Oct. 2019, https://pagesix.com/2019/10/01/why-angelina-jolie-wore-her-iconic-leg-baring-2012-oscars-dress/.

p. 126: "I was going to wear my swan": "Martin Tries at Dull Oscars," BBC, 26 Mar. 2001, news.bbc.co.uk, http://news.bbc.co.uk/2/hi/entertainment/1242902.stm.

p. 127: "It was really funny": "Björk Again," *Times*, https://www.thetimes.co.uk/article/bjork-again-2d37mrbvphv, accessed 28 Nov. 2020.

p. 127: "They were almost going to put": Isaac Guzmán, "Björk Is Your Tour Guide: Her Stories About the MOMA Exhibit," *Time*, https://time.com/3731906/bjork-moma-retrospective/, accessed 28 Nov. 2020.

p. 127: "reflects a certain independent spirit": Matthew Schneier, "The Most Famous Macedonian Designer You've Never Heard Of (Pub-lished 2015)," *New York Times*, 11 Feb. 2015, https://www.nytimes.com/2015/02/12/fashion/the-most-famous-macedonian-designer-youve-never-heard-of.html.

P. 128: It was birdbrained of her: Cruz, Clarissa, Alice M. Lee, and Megan Quit-kin. "The Fashions," *Entertainment Weekly*, 6 April 2001, 60.

p. 128: Even as it has risen: "Oscars' 10 Worst Dressed Stars Ever: Björk, Gwyneth Paltrow and More," E! Online, 23 Feb. 2013, https://www.eon-line.com/news/391035/oscars-10-worst-dressed-stars-ever-bjork-gwyn-eth-paltrow-and-more.

p. 128: "With the Oscars, there's a uniform": "3 Infamous Oscar Dresses Remembered by the Designers," *Hollywood Reporter*, https://www.holly-woodreporter.com/news/oscars-3-infamous-dresses-775363, accessed 29 Nov. 2020.

p. 129: But the true star: "Titanic" Fakes," *Entertainment Weekly*, https://ew.com/article/1998/04/10/titanic-fakes/, accessed 13 Feb. 2021.

p. 130: Inspired by the film: "Céline Dion Wore the Titanic 'Heart of the Ocean' Necklace by Vetements," *Vogue Paris*, https://www.vogue.fr/jewelry/article/celine-dion-wore-the-titanic-heart-of-the-ocean-necklace-by-ve-tements, accessed 11 Apr. 2021.

p. 130: The next year: Michelle Ruiz, "Best Oscars Ever? 1999, Hands Down," *Vogue*, https://www.vogue.com/article/1999-best-oscars-ever, accessed 13 Feb. 2021.

p. 130: The rapper himself: Steve Pond, *The Big Show: High Times and Dirty Dealings Backstage at the Academy Awards* (New York: Farrar, Straus and Giroux, 2005).

p. 131: "un-celebrity like": "Eminem Gives Oscar Thanks," E! Online, 25 Mar. 2003, https://www.eonline.com/news/44849/eminem-gives-oscar-thanks.

p. 131: "traumatizing": "'I Have a Sense of Urgency': Sufjan Stevens Wakes from the American Dream," *Guardian*, 25 Sept. 2020, http://www.theguardian.com/music/2020/sep/25/sufjan-stevens-interview-the-ascension.

p. 131: His look was celebrated: Twitter, https://twitter.com/i/events/970711685630742529, accessed 13 Feb. 2021.

p. 134: The Lebanon-based Elie Saab: Ashley Simpson, "Halle Berry Jump-started Elie Saab's Career," *CR Fashion Book*, 14 Aug. 2019, https://www.crfashionbook.com/celebrity/a28648416/halle-berry-elie-saab-oscars-red-carpet/.

p. 134: "I saw so many gowns": Michael Quintanilla, "Flesh and Some Flash," *Los Angeles Times*, 25 Mar. 2002, 66.

p. 134: "People always wanting": Ramin Setoodeh, "How Halle Berry Fought Her Way to the Director's Chair," *Variety*, 9 Sept. 2020, https://variety.com/2020/film/news/halle-berry-bruised-directing-toronto-film-festival-1234762255/.

p. 135: "proves herself to be": A. O. Scott, "FILM REVIEW; Courtesy and Decency Play Sneaky With a Tough Guy (Published 2001)," *New York Times*, 26 Dec. 2001, https://www.nytimes.com/2001/12/26/movies/film-review-courtesy-and-decency-play-sneaky-with-a-tough-guy.html.

p. 135: "The film's only flaw": Roger Ebert, "Monster's Ball Movie Review & Film Summary (2002) | Roger Ebert," https://www.rogerebert.com/reviews/monsters-ball-2002, accessed 3 Jan. 2021.

p. 135: "I couldn't do that": "Angela Bassett Slams Halle Berry's Oscar Role," *Entertainment Weekly*, https://ew.com/article/2002/06/24/angela-bassett-slams-halle-berrys-oscar-role/, accessed 4 Jan. 2021.

p. 136: "silly and puerile": "A Well-Deserved Oscar for an Ill-Conceived Movie," *Baltimore Sun*, https://webcache.googleusercontent.com/search?q=cache:zvHXTpE2B0QJ:https://www.baltimoresun.com/news/bs-xpm-2002-03-27-0203270093-story.html+&cd=20&hl=en&ct=clnk&gl=us, accessed 4 Jan. 2021.

p. 136: "I didn't feel it was exploitative": Ramin Setoodeh, "How Halle Berry Fought Her Way to the Director's Chair," *Variety*, 9 Sept. 2020, https://variety.com/2020/film/news/halle-berry-bruised-directing-toronto-film-festival-1234762255/.

p. 136: "A lot of things happen": "Halle Berry Talks about Sex, Scandal and Success," *Guardian*, 3 June 2002, http://www.theguardian.com/culture/2002/jun/03/artsfeatures.

p. 137: "I thought 'Oh, all these great scripts'": Ramin Setoodeh, "How Halle Berry Fought Her Way to the Director's Chair," *Variety*, 9 Sept. 2020, https://variety.com/2020/film/news/halle-berry-bruised-directing-toronto-film-festival-1234762255/.

p. 137: "Halle Berry made the name": Farouk Chekoufi, "Lebanese Designer Elie Saab on Haute Couture and How Halle Berry Changed His Business," *Vogue Australia*, 16 July 2019, https://www.vogue.com.au/fashion/news/lebanese-designer-elie-saab-on-haute-couture-and-how-halle-berry-changed-his-business/news-story/39833c9232721d6d5feb4fc781349779.

p. 139: Williams appeared in productions: "Michelle Williams Climbs 'Brokeback Mountain,'" *Entertainment Weekly*, https://ew.com/article/2006/01/06/michelle-williams-climbs-brokeback-mountain/, accessed 24 Jan. 2021.

p. 140: Wang and Williams: Katherine E. Krohn, *Vera Wang: Enduring Style* (Minneapolis: Twenty-First Century Books, 2009), 41.

p. 141: "never gave up on love": Amanda Fortini, "Cover Story: Michelle Williams on Her Private Wedding and Public Fight for Equal Pay," *Vanity Fair*, https://www.vanityfair.com/hollywood/2018/07/michelle-williams-marriage-wedding-equal-pay, accessed 27 Jan. 2021.

p. 142: "All tips to make you look thin": "Pregnant at the Oscars? Stars, Producers Reveal How to Dress," *Hollywood Reporter*, 22 Feb. 2019, https://www.hollywoodreporter.com/news/pregnant-at-oscars-stars-producers-reveal-how-dress-1186748.

p. 143: "looked like she may have been": "Queen Latifah and Catherine Zeta-Jones Had a Memorable Oscar Moment," *Entertainment Weekly*, https://ew.com/article/2003/03/24/queen-latifah-and-catherine-zeta-jones-had-memorable-oscar-moment/, accessed 5 Feb. 2021.

p. 144: "ripe": "Dressing for the Oscars," 24 Mar. 2003, BBC, http://news.bbc.co.uk/2/hi/entertainment/2881483.stm.

p. 144: "magnificently pregnant": Patteson, Jean. "Black remained prominent," *Orlando Sentinel,* 24 Mar. 2003, C5.

p. 144: "pregnancy style": "Natalie Portman's Pregnancy Style," https://www.cbsnews.com/pictures/natalie-portmans-pregnancy-style/, accessed 5 Feb. 2021.

p. 144: "defies you to argue": "Oscars: Natalie Portman and the Anatomy of a Dress," *LA Times Blogs*—Ministry of Gossip, 27 Feb. 2011, https://latimesblogs.latimes.com/gossip/2011/02/oscars-natalie-portman-and-the-anatomy-of-a-dress.html.

p. 144: "sported flushed cheeks": "Oscars Red Carpet 2011 - Natalie Portman," *People*, https://people.com/awards/oscars-red-carpet-2011-natalie-portman/, accessed 5 Feb. 2021.

p. 145: "staying at home": "Pregnant Natalie Portman Pulls out of Oscars," AP, 25 Feb. 2017, https://apnews.com/article/9214fd0798514bf28bf-43819f9eeeedd.

p. 145: But it's similarly telling: Hannah Seligson, "This Is the TV Ad the Oscars Didn't Allow On Air," *New York Times*, 19 Feb. 2020, https://www.nytimes.com/2020/02/19/us/postpartum-ad-oscars-frida.html.

p. 146: the last time a woman triumphed: "Oscars Reminder: No Woman Has Won a Screenplay Award in 12 Years," *Los Angeles Times*, 10 Feb. 2020, https://www.latimes.com/entertainment-arts/movies/story/2020-02-09/oscars-2020-screenplay-women-writers.

p. 148: "If 'Jezebel' were a person": "Dear Diablo Cody: I Wish My Boyfriend's Junk Smelled Like Pie," *Jezebel*, https://jezebel.com/dear-diablo-cody-i-wish-my-boyfriends-junk-smelled-lik-328540, accessed 17 Jan. 2021.

p. 149: "I've met so many hyperarticulate": "Diablo Cody: From Ex-Stripper to A-Lister," *Entertainment Weekly*, https://ew.com/article/2007/11/05/juno-makes-ex-stripper-hollywood-lister/, accessed 17 Jan. 2021.

p. 149: "wrote her own Wikipedia": David Carr, "Diablo Cody: Climbing the Stripper Pole to Hollywood Stardom (Published 2007)," *New York Times*, 3 Dec. 2007, https://www.nytimes.com/2007/12/03/arts/03i-ht-juno.1.8567521.html.

p. 150: "The diamond collar": Molly Friedman, "Oscars 2008: Top Seven Most Cringeworthy Ensembles," *Gawker*, http://gawker.com/360212/oscars-2008-top-seven-most-cringeworthy-ensembles, accessed 17 Jan. 2021.

p. 150: A writer over at: Oscar Look Book...So I'm an Oscar Whore, So What? At the Amoeblog. 24 Mar. 2018, https://web.archive.org/web/20180324230817/https://www.amoeba.com/blog/2008/02/all-the-news-that-s-fit-to-sing/oscar-look-book-so-i-m-an-oscar-whore-so-what-.html.

p. 150: "As for Diablo Cody": Dana Stevens, "Diablo 'Pebbles' Cody," *Slate Magazine*, 25 Feb. 2008, https://slate.com/news-and-politics/2008/02/oscars-2008-diablo-pebbles-cody.html.

p. 151: the pattern's history: Colette Shade, "The Trashy, Expensive, Contradictory Reputation of Leopard Print," *Racked*, 7 Mar. 2018, https://www.racked.com/2018/3/7/17053964/leopard-print-history.

p. 152: "Uh, you're a stripper/screenwriter": "Oscar-Winner Diablo Cody: The Latest Victim Of Girl-On-Girl Crime," *Jezebel*, https://jezebel.com/oscar-winner-diablo-cody-the-latest-victim-of-girl-on-361321, accessed 17 Jan. 2021.

p. 152: And because she used to strip: "NSFW: Diablo Cody Nude," */Film*, 26 Feb. 2008, https://www.slashfilm.com/nsfw-diablo-cody-nude/.

p. 152: "After all, one glance": Diablo Cody's Nude Pics Hit the Web [NSFW]. 8 May 2018, https://web.archive.org/web/20180508055930/https://film-schoolrejects.com/diablo-codys-nude-pics-hit-the-web-nsfw/.

p. 155: "Desk-job ambitions": Jake Mooney, "The Audition That Left Them Speechless (Published 2007)," *New York Times*, 9 Dec. 2007, https://www.nytimes.com/2007/12/09/nyregion/thecity/09disp.html.

p. 155: "Just for the record": "Meet Gabby Sidibe, the Star of Precious," *Guardian*, 20 Jan. 2010, http://www.theguardian.com/film/2010/jan/20/gab-by-sidibe-precious.

p. 156: "[She] so completely creates": Alex Jung, "Gabourey Sidibe Is Not Precious Jones; Creates Pandemonium," *Colorlines*, 27 Jan. 2010, https://www.colorlines.com/articles/gabourey-sidibe-not-precious-jones-cre-ates-pandemonium.

p. 156: "I was told": Gabourey Sidibe, *This Is Just My Face: Try Not to Stare* (New York: Vintage Detail, 2018), 74.

p. 157: "I don't need a dress": Gabourey Sidibe, *This Is Just My Face: Try Not to Stare* (New York: Vintage Detail, 2018), 77.

p. 157: headlines like "Gabourey Sidibe's Dress Mystery": Hollie McKay, "Gabourey Sidibe's Dress Mystery: When Plus Size Is Too Big for Hollywood," *Fox News*, 26 Mar. 2015, https://www.foxnews.com/entertainment/gabourey-sidibes-dress-mystery-when-plus-size-is-too-big-for-hollywood.

p. 157: "Gabby's Red Carpet": "Gabby's Red Carpet Presence Sparks Plus-Size Debate," *Essence*, https://www.essence.com/news/as-we-watch-zaftig-and-proud-actress/, accessed 18 Jan. 2021.

p. 157: "A woman with curves": Meredith Stebbins, "What Will the Best-Actress Nominees Wear on Oscar Night?" *Vanity Fair*, https://www.vanityfair.com/news/2010/03/dream-dresses-for-oscar-night, accessed 18 Jan. 2021.

p. 158: "We've been offered": "Designers Vie to Dress 'full-Sized' Gabourey Sidibe," *USA Today*, http://content.usatoday.com/communities/enter-tainment/post/2010/02/designers-vye-to-dress-full-sized-gabourey-sidibe/1, accessed 18 Jan. 2021.

p. 158: "I hate to say it": Hollie McKay, "Gabourey Sidibe's Dress Mystery: When Plus Size Is Too Big for Hollywood," *Fox News*, 26 Mar. 2015, https://www.foxnews.com/entertainment/gabourey-sidibes-dress-mys-tery-when-plus-size-is-too-big-for-hollywood.

p. 158: "This is some reeeeal funny style": "Gabourey Sidibe's Oscar Dress Mess," *Salon*, 8 Mar. 2010, https://www.salon.com/2010/03/07/gabourey_sidibe_oscars_open2010/.

p. 159: "Gabourey looked like a red-carpet queen": Hayley Phelan, "10 Best Dressed at the 2010 Oscars," *Teen Vogue*, https://www.teenvogue.com/gallery/best-dressed-oscars-2010, accessed 18 Jan. 2021.

p. 159: Just days after the Oscars: "Can Talent Outweigh Size in Hollywood?" *CNN*, http://www.cnn.com/2010/SHOWBIZ/Movies/03/10/gabourey. sidibe.career/index.html, accessed 18 Jan. 2021.

p. 159: the bigger issue was racism: Margot Magowan, "Gabourey Sidibe Isn't Too Fat for Hollywood, She's Too Black," City Brights: Margot Magowan, 14 Mar. 2010, https://blog.sfgate.com/mmagowan/2010/03/14/ gabourey-sidibe-isnt-too-fat-for-hollywood-shes-too-black/.

p. 159: By the end of the month: "Enough About Sidibe's Weight, Already," *Jezebel*, https://jezebel.com/enough-about-sidibes-weight-al- ready-5502657, accessed 18 Jan. 2021.

p. 160: "We may have the same face": Gabourey Sidibe, *This Is Just My Face: Try Not to Star*e (New York: Vintage Detail, 2018), 2.

p. 163: BuzzFeed published a post: Louis Peitzman, "Why Do People Hate Anne Hathaway?" *BuzzFeed*, https://www.buzzfeed.com/louispeitzman/ why-do-people-hate-anne-hathaway, accessed 30 Oct. 2020.

p. 163: In February the next year: Brian Moylan, "Why Does Everyone Hate Anne Hathaway?" *Hollywood.Com*, 8 Feb. 2013, http://www.hollywood. com/celebrities/why-do-people-hate-anne-hathaway-60231034/.

p. 163: Even I joined in: Esther Zuckerman, "Anne Hathaway Will Be This Annoying at the Oscars," *Atlantic*, 22 Feb. 2013, https://www.theatlantic. com/culture/archive/2013/02/anne-hathaway-oscars-2013/318067/.

p. 164: "a pink embroidered tulle": "Anne Hathaway Oscar Dress Switch: Why She Snubbed Valentino," *Us Weekly*, 26 Feb. 2013, https://www.usmag- azine.com/stylish/news/anne-hathaway-oscar-dress-switch-why-she- ditched-a-stunning-valentino-gown-last-minute-2013262/.

p. 164: "Anyone else feeling": "Https://Twitter.Com/Hathawaynipple." Twitter, https://twitter.com/hathawaynipple, accessed 1 Nov. 2020.

p. 164: "I tried on a ton": "Anne Hathaway Apologizes for Last-Minute Oscar Gown Switch," *TODAY*, http://www.today.com/style/anne-hathaway-apol- ogizes-last-minute-oscar-gown-switch-1C8567262, accessed 1 Nov. 2020.

p. 166: "I can't figure out": Ann Friedman, "Why Do Women Hate Anne Hathaway (But Love Jennifer Lawrence)?" *The Cut*, https://www.thecut. com/2013/02/why-do-women-hate-hathaway-but-love-lawrence.html, accessed 30 Oct. 2020.

p. 166: Her costar Amanda Seyfried: "Anne Hathaway Oscar Dress Switch: Why She Snubbed Valentino," *Us Weekly*, 26 Feb. 2013, https://www. usmagazine.com/stylish/news/anne-hathaway-oscar-dress-switch-why- she-ditched-a-stunning-valentino-gown-last-minute-2013262/.

p. 166: "It came to my attention: "Anne Hathaway Apologized for That Prada Oscars Dress," *The Cut*, https://www.thecut.com/2013/02/anne-hatha- way-sorry-about-her-prada-oscars-dress.html, accessed 1 Nov. 2020.

p. 168: "Nairobi blue": Caitlin Morton, "Lupita Nyong'o Stuns In 'Nairobi Blue' Prada At 2014 Academy Awards," *MTV News*, http://www.mtv.com/news/2520371/lupita-nyongo-nairobi-blue-academy-awards/, accessed 27 Dec. 2020.

p. 168: "It's a blue that reminds me": "Lupita Nyong'o Wears Prada to the 2014 Oscars: 'It's A Blue That Reminds Me of Nairobi,'" E! Online, 3 Mar. 2014, https://www.eonline.com/news/516472/lupita-nyong-o-wears-prada-to-the-2014-oscars-it-s-a-blue-that-reminds-me-of-nairobi.

p. 170: Shortly after the movie debuted: "Toronto: Your Best Picture Winner Will Be 12 Years a Slave," *Vulture*, https://www.vulture.com/2013/09/12-years-a-slave-will-win-best-picture.html, accessed 27 Dec. 2020.

p. 170: She linked up with: Hamish Bowles, "Lupita Nyong'o on Winning the Oscar, Becoming the Face of Lancôme, and Her First Cover of Vogue," *Vogue*, https://www.vogue.com/article/lupita-nyongo-first-vogue-cover, accessed 27 Dec. 2020.

p. 170: "When I knew": Marlow Stern, "Lupita Nyong'o Discusses Her Style Inspirations and Red Carpet Fashion," *Daily Beast*, 24 Feb. 2014, https://www.thedailybeast.com/articles/2014/02/24/lupita-nyong-o-discusses-her-style-inspirations-and-red-carpet-fashion.

p. 171: "impresses on the red carpet": Stuart Emmrich, "Lupita Nyong'o Impresses on the Red Carpet (Published 2013)," *New York Times*, 15 Nov. 2013, https://www.nytimes.com/2013/11/17/fashion/Lupita-Nyongo-fashion-Impresses-on-the-Red-Carpet.html.

p. 171: "My complexion had always been": "Read Lupita Nyongos Moving ESSENCE Speech," *Vulture*, https://www.vulture.com/2014/02/read-lupita-nyongs-moving-essence-speech.html, accessed 28 Dec. 2020.

p. 172: She was labeled: "Lupita Nyong'o's Stirring Message: Dark Skin Is Beautiful," *ABC News*, https://abcnews.go.com/Entertainment/lupita-nyongos-stirring-message-dark-skin-beautiful/story?id=23456925, accessed 28 Dec. 2020.

p. 172: *Vanity Fair* was accused: Emma Barker, "Did Vanity Fair Lighten Lupita Nyong'o's Skin Color?" *Cosmopolitan*, 17 Jan. 2014, https://www.cosmopolitan.com/celebrity/news/lupita-nyongo-vanity-fair-retouching.

p. 172: Some argued that: Noah Berlatsky, "Lupita Nyong'o's Radical, World-Changing Style," *The Atlantic*, 6 Mar. 2014, https://www.theatlantic.com/entertainment/archive/2014/03/lupita-nyongos-radical-world-changing-style/284274/.

p. 172: "Her face everywhere": "Lupita Nyong'o Is Everywhere Right Now. We Need More Faces Like Hers." *Jezebel*, https://jezebel.com/lupita-nyongo-is-everywhere-right-now-we-need-more-fa-1517374173, accessed 28 Dec. 2020.

p. 173: "Vashti chose to put her": Instagram, https://www.instagram.com/accounts/login/?next=/p/B3maSxiJr3u/, accessed 28 Dec. 2020.

p. 175: She was there to claim: Abby Aguirre, "Zendaya Talks Spider-Man, Her First Love, and Reinventing Disney Stardom," *Vogue*, https://www.vogue.com/article/zendaya-interview-july-vogue-cover-spider-man-homecoming, accessed 5 Dec. 2020.

p. 175: Zendaya posted a side by side: Instagram, https://www.instagram.com/accounts/login/?next=/p/zbilNtpmOO/, accessed 5 Dec. 2020.

p. 176: "If you didn't know": Alessandra Codinha, "Zendaya Is This Academy Awards' Breakout Style Star," *Vogue*, https://www.vogue.com/article/zendaya-oscars-2015-dress-vivienne-westwood, accessed 5 Dec. 2020.

p. 177: "There is already harsh criticism": "Zendaya-Giuliana Rancic Dreadlocks Dispute: Ava DuVernay, Kerry Washington, Whoopi Goldberg Back Disney Star," *Hollywood Reporter*, https://www.hollywoodreporter.com/news/zendaya-giuliana-rancic-dreadlocks-dispute-777418, accessed 6 Dec. 2020.

p. 177: Rancic scrambled: "Giuliana Rancic Blames Editing Mishap for Zendaya Storm," *Time*, https://time.com/3772300/giuliana-rancic-zendaya-edited/, accessed 6 Dec. 2020.

p. 178: That very same year: Reggie Ugwu, "The Hashtag That Changed the Oscars: An Oral History," *New York Times*, 6 Feb. 2020, https://www.nytimes.com/2020/02/06/movies/oscarssowhite-history.html.

p. 178: Unless you were following: Abby Aguirre, "Zendaya Talks Spider-Man, Her First Love, and Reinventing Disney Stardom," *Vogue*, https://www.vogue.com/article/zendaya-interview-july-vogue-cover-spider-man-homecoming, accessed 6 Dec. 2020.

p. 180: "Your ass is mine": Patricia Garcia, "A History of the Mani Cam: The Red Carpet's Most Divisive Gimmick," *Vogue*, https://www.vogue.com/article/mani-cam-history-best-worst-moments, accessed 15 Feb. 2021.

p. 181: "humiliating": Laura Brown, "April Cover Story: The Moore The Better," *Harper's BAZAAR*, 11 Mar. 2015, https://www.harpersbazaar.com/culture/features/a10224/julianne-moore-0415/.

p. 182: The viral video: Megan Friedman, "Alejandro González Iñárritu *Did* Clap for Winner Jenny Beavan at the Oscars, Thinks She's 'Very Deserving,'" *Marie Claire*, 29 Feb. 2016, https://www.marieclaire.com/culture/news/a18958/jenny-beavan-oscars-vine/.

p. 182: "I've learned a lot": "Alejandro G. Iñárritu Sets Record Straight on Jenny Beavan Vine," *Entertainment Weekly*, https://ew.com/article/2016/03/03/alejandro-inarritu-jenny-beavan-vine/, accessed 29 Nov. 2020.

p. 184: "I think it may have said": "'Mad Max' Costume Designer Jenny Beavan on Her Oscar Win: 'I Don't Mind in the Least If They Didn't Clap,'" *Hollywood Reporter*, https://www.hollywoodreporter.com/news/mad-max-costume-designer-jenny-872342, accessed 30 Nov. 2020.

p. 184: She saw the outfit as a tip: "'Mad Max' Costume Designer Jenny Beavan on Her Oscar Win: 'I Don't Mind in the Least If They Didn't Clap,'" *Hollywood Reporter*, https://www.hollywoodreporter.com/news/mad-max-costume-designer-jenny-872342, accessed 1 Dec. 2020.

p. 185: "oily rag": "Jenny Beavan: 'There Was Cate Blanchett Looking like an Angel, and Me Looking like a Biker,'" *Guardian*, 20 Mar. 2016, http://www.theguardian.com/lifeandstyle/2016/mar/20/interview-jenny-beavan-costume-designer-oscars.

p. 185: "The thing that lots": "Jenny Beavan: 'There Was Cate Blanchett Looking like an Angel, and Me Looking like a Biker,'" *Guardian*, 20 Mar. 2016, http://www.theguardian.com/lifeandstyle/2016/mar/20/interview-jenny-beavan-costume-designer-oscars.

p. 185: In 2020, legendary designer Sandy Powell: Christian Allaire, "Sandy Powell's Oscars Suit Will Honor a Good Cause," *Vogue*, https://www.vogue.com/vogueworld/article/sandy-powell-baftas-oscars-suit-derek-jerman, accessed 1 Dec. 2020.

p. 185: Ruth E. Carter, who became: "Ruth E. Carter Makes History as First Black Woman to Win Best Costume Design at Oscars 2019," *People*, https://people.com/movies/oscars-2019-ruth-carter-first-black-woman-win-best-costume-design/, accessed 1 Dec. 2020.

p. 186: "bag lady": Benjamin Lee, "Stephen Fry Deletes Twitter Account after Baftas 'bag Lady' Criticism," *Guardian*, 15 Feb. 2016, https://www.theguardian.com/film/2016/feb/15/stephen-fry-deletes-twitter-account-after-baftas-bag-lady-offence.

p. 186: "looked repelled": "Opinion | The Men of the Oscars Humiliate a Brilliant Woman: Mallick," *Toronto Star*, 2 Mar. 2016, https://www.thestar.com/opinion/commentary/2016/03/02/the-men-of-the-oscars-humiliate-a-brilliant-woman-mallick.html.

p. 189: The likes of Sidney Poitier: Jonathan Evans, "From McQueen to Momoa: These Are the Most Stylish Men in Oscars History," *Esquire*, 30 Jan. 2020, https://www.esquire.com/style/mens-fashion/g26379698/oscars-best-dressed-men-academy-awards/.

p. 189: "worst-dressed men of all-time": "The Worst-Dressed Men at the Oscars . . . Ever." *GQ*, https://www.gq.com/gallery/oscars-academy-awards-worst-dressed-men-of-all-time, accessed 6 Feb. 2021.

p. 190: "I think fashion is all about": Twitter, https://twitter.com/adamrippon/status/970815284176068609, accessed 7 Feb. 2021.

p. 191: Both were softer: "How the Bondage Harness Was Rebranded as Red Carpet-Wear," *Guardian*, 28 Jan. 2019, http://www.theguardian.com/world/shortcuts/2019/jan/28/sex-harness-red-carpet.

p. 192: *Black Panther* had come out: "Box Office: 'Black Panther' Becomes Top-Grossing Superhero Film of All Time in U.S." *Hollywood Reporter*, 24 Mar. 2018, https://www.hollywoodreporter.com/heat-vision/box-office-black-panther-becomes-top-grossing-superhero-film-all-time-us-1097101.

p. 192: Attending as a presenter: Matt Sebra, "The Best-Dressed Men on the Oscars 2018 Red Carpet," *GQ*, https://www.gq.com/gallery/oscars-2018-best-dressed-men, accessed 7 Feb. 2021.

p. 192: "Chadwick Boseman": "Chadwick Boseman Was the King of the Oscars Red Carpet," *Fader*, https://www.thefader.com/2018/03/04/chadwick-boseman-oscars-red-carpet, accessed 7 Feb. 2021.

p. 192: Another echoed: "Chadwick Boseman's Jacket Is King of the 2018 Oscars Red Carpet," E! Online, 5 Mar. 2018, https://www.eonline.com/news/918062/chadwick-boseman-s-jacket-is-king-of-the-2018-oscars-red-carpet.

p. 192: But it wasn't just: Kristina Rodulfo, "Chadwick Boseman Shouted 'Wakanda Forever!' On the Oscars Red Carpet." *Elle*, 5 Mar. 2018, https://www.elle.com/culture/a19078409/chadwick-boseman-oscars-2018-red-carpet-wakanda/.

p. 193: "Men are eager": Rachel Tashjian, "How the 2019 Oscars Rewrote the Rules for Men on the Red Carpet," *GQ*, https://www.gq.com/story/2019-oscars-style-was-pretty-great, accessed 29 May 2021.

p. 196: "Chloé Zhao Proves": Alexis Bennett, "White Sneakers You Can Wear Everywhere, Inspired by Chloé Zhao's Chic 2021 Oscars Look," *Vogue*, https://www.vogue.com/slideshow/white-sneakers-chloe-zhao-oscars, accessed 6 May 2021.

p. 196: Going into the night: Nicholas Barber, "At Cannes, Wear Heels and Don't Take Selfies," *The New York Times*, https://www.nytimes.com/2019/05/13/arts/the-rules-of-cannes.html, accessed 13 May 2019.

index

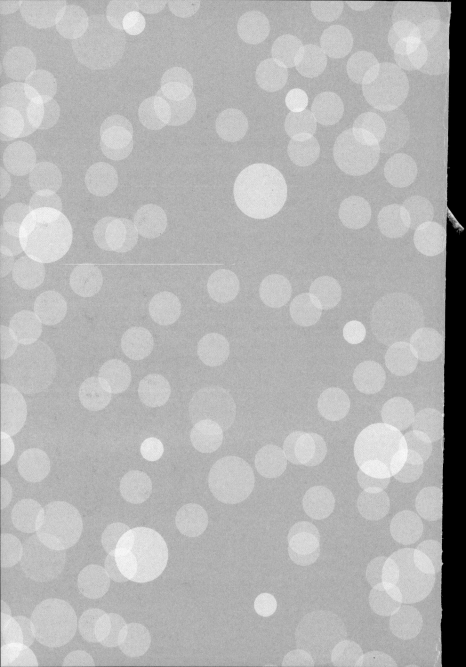